BLACK DOUGLAS

To
H. K. D. and P. M. M. D.

THE BLACK DOUGLAS

I. M. Davis

The good lord of Douglas
In whom all wit and worship was
Scottish chronicler

James Douglas, always bent on plots
English chronicler

Routledge & Kegan Paul
London and Boston

First published in 1974
by Routledge & Kegan Paul Ltd
Broadway House, 68–74 Carter Lane,
London EC4V 5EL and
9 Park Street,
Boston, Mass. 02108, U.S.A.
Printed in Great Britain by
T. & A. Constable Ltd, Edinburgh
© I. M. Davis 1974
No part of this book may be reproduced in
any form without permission from the
publisher, except for the quotation of brief
passages in criticism

ISBN 0 7100 7753 X

Contents

		page
	Map: Southern Scotland and Northern England in the Fourteenth Century	vi
	Prologue: Audience before Stirling	1
1	The Disinherited	7
2	The Disastrous Year	16
3	Douglas Regained	31
4	The Fortresses Fall	53
5	Bannockburn	67
6	Fortis Malleator Anglorum	82
7	Sorts of Traitors	98
8	The Truce that Failed	122
9	The Perfection of a General's Skill	129
10	The Reign Fulfilled	147
11	The Last Commission	155
	Appendix 1: The Myth of the Thrown Heart	166
	Appendix 2: Genealogy of the Douglas Family in the Thirteenth and Fourteenth Centuries	169
	Sources	172
	Bibliography	177
	Index	179

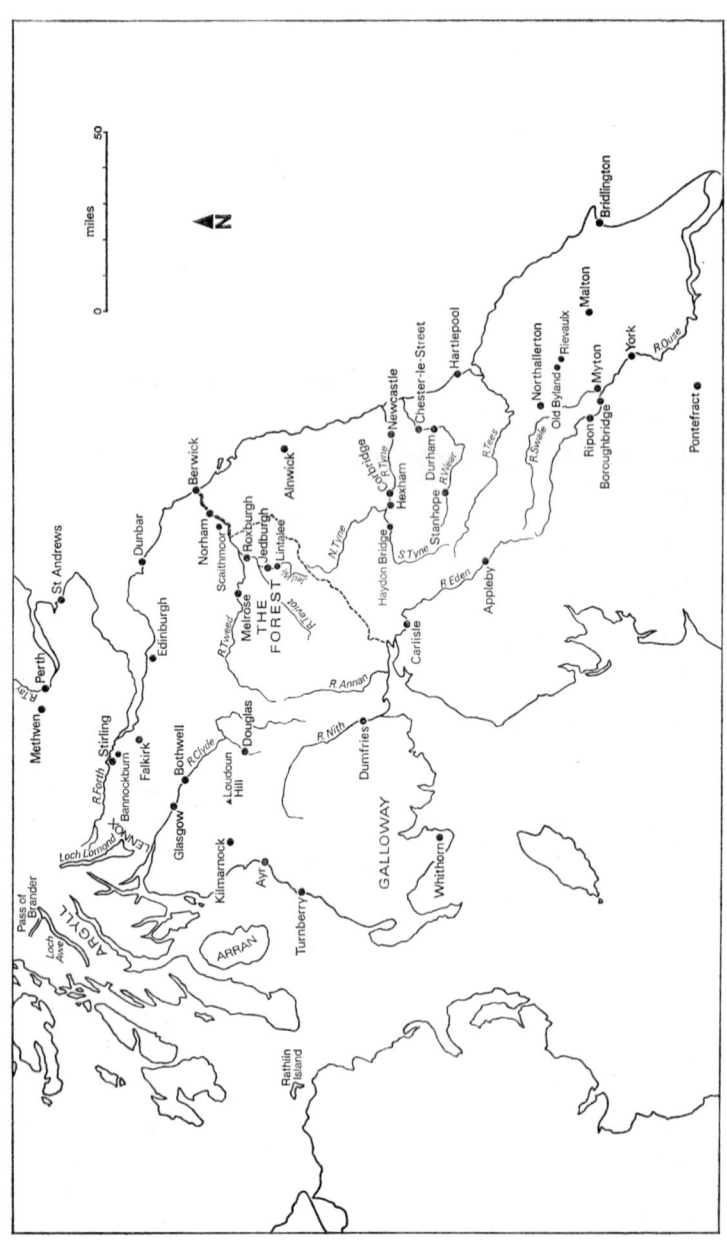

Southern Scotland and Northern England in the Fourteenth Century

Prologue

Audience before Stirling

> When Alysander our King was dede,
> That Scotland led in love and lee,
> Away was sons of ale and brede,
> Of wine and wax, gamyn and glee;
> Our gold was changed into lede.
> Christ born into Virginitie,
> Succour Scotland and remede
> That stayed is in perplexitie.
>
> Anon.

In May 1304, King Edward of England, sitting in his palatial camp before Stirling Castle, could contemplate a major undertaking all but complete. When the castle he was now besieging fell, the separate kingdom of Scotland would have ceased to exist, and his writ would run from Cornwall to Caithness.

Gratifyingly, the enterprise had been accomplished with the strict regard to legality on which he prided himself. It had been rendered possible through the death fourteen years earlier of the seven-year-old girl who was Queen of Scotland, the granddaughter of Alexander III, last king of the direct line of Macalpine. On her succession Edward had secured her betrothal to his heir, envisaging the union of the kingdoms on his own death, but hers, rendering as it did the crown of Scotland the objective of a dozen claimants kin to former sovereigns, had opened a quicker way. The unquestionable front-runners among these claimants had been two Scottish noblemen, Bruce of Annandale and Balliol of Galloway, whose claims and whose powers were so dangerously near that the representatives of the kingdom, in a praiseworthy attempt to avert civil war, had resolved and secured the claimants' agreement that the succession should be adjudicated by an outside authority. This role they had asked Edward to assume. Naturally he had agreed, and no less naturally had stipulated as his price recognition, by the Scots and by the claimants, of the English kings' traditional claim—which he had never formerly pressed and Alexander had never acknowledged— to overlordship of Scotland; he had been careful to allay Scottish fears by declaring that he required no more than homage and the rights attendant thereon, and equally careful to leave these rights undefined. Only when, his condition accepted and his judgment given in favour of John Balliol, the new King of Scots had done homage to him, had Edward let it be known that his interpretation of the rights attendant on homage included the oversight of Scottish justice, the direction of Scottish international relationships and the benefit of military service from the Scots.

His undertaking might have been completed there. He had manoeuvred the Scots into a heads-I-win tails-you-lose situation whereby compliance with his demands gave him adequate control of Scotland no less than of England, resistance to them an entitlement, in his own eyes, to claim the kingdom as forfeited by a disloyal vassal. Balliol, a pliant man, would probably have been content to reign on Edward's terms, but his subjects preferred independence, and in 1295, on Edward's embroilment in war with France, the Scottish magnates had coerced their king into defiance of his overlord. Afforded, as he saw it, just occasion to annex the realm, Edward had acted at once. A few months in 1296 had sufficed for the conquest that, accelerated perhaps by horror at the massacre of Berwick, where on the town's quick capture Edward had let his troops slaughter without mercy for age or sex, had ended in the deposition of Balliol and the incorporation of Scotland in the Plantagenet dominions.

That victory, in fact, had been too quick, leaving the Scots less conquered than concussed. Edward's departure from his acquisition had been followed almost at once by the first of the sporadic uprisings that, gaining in strength and cohesion, had by 1297 developed into the insurrection that culminated in the defeat of the English at Stirling Bridge by William Wallace and Andrew Murray. Though at Falkirk the following year Edward had avenged that humiliation, the maintenance of war on two fronts had precluded the sustained effort necessary to subjugate the Scots until the defeat of the French by Edward's Flemish allies at Courtrai in 1302 had opened the way to a satisfactory settlement with France, and thence to the completion of his grand design for Scotland. Now it was all but achieved, with the starving, hopeless garrison of Stirling Castle the last defenders of Scottish independence left in the field.

As he awaited their surrender Edward received the homage of the conquered Scots. He had identified by now his mistake of 1296, when by appointing Englishmen to local and national offices in Scotland he had made nakedly plain to Scotsmen the imposition upon them of English rule, and he would not repeat it. In future his commands must be acceptably transmitted to the Scottish people through magnates and officials of their own blood, a necessity which meant restoring to those Scottish leaders who admitted his sovereignty the forfeited possessions whence they derived their influence. The earl of Buchan, kinsman of John Balliol, head of the powerful house of Comyn and long one of the principal Scottish commanders, was restored to his earldom. Sir Ingram Umfraville, who had served as Guardian, or regent, of Scotland in Balliol's name, was permitted to redeem his estates at five years' purchase; James the Steward of Scotland, throughout the war one of the most persistent opponents of the English, at a lesser sum; and like terms were offered all magnates who might serve to reconcile their people to English rule. This politic clemency, however, extended only to those who were able and appeared willing to promote Edward's authority in Scotland; William Wallace had been called on to surrender without guarantee of life or freedom.

Among those already received to Edward's fealty was William Lamberton, bishop of St Andrews, who on performing homage had at once been restored to his temporalities. This prelate had been Scotland's foremost diplomat, the negotiator with Philip of France of the Franco-Scottish treaty of 1301 (abandoned by Philip when adherence to it no longer suited him) whereby each ally swore to make no peace with Edward in which the other was not included, but as the incumbent of the premier see of Scotland he was very much a man to be won over. Quick in fact to proffer homage to Edward on Scotland's defeat, Lamberton had passed beyond mere acceptance with the English king. A clever, sinuous man with remarkable powers of persuasion, he was already contriving so to ingratiate himself that Edward would later describe him as 'one in whom he trusted above all others in the realm of Scotland'.* Thus when Lamberton appeared at the royal pavilion with a young squire for whom he sought acceptance as Edward's vassal, he was readily admitted. He came before the king, leading with him the dark, long-legged boy who was his protégé.

His name was James, he was about eighteen years old, and he was the eldest son of William 'le Hardi', late lord of Douglas in Lanarkshire. This nobleman had in the first year of the war been active if not particularly effective in the cause of independence. Appointed governor of Berwick Castle at the outbreak of war, he had—perhaps unnerved by the massacre he witnessed from its walls on the town's capture—been quick to surrender to Edward, and a few months later had been one of the many Scottish nobles and gentry to pay homage to the English king; yet in the spring of 1297 he had been the first Scottish nobleman to join William Wallace in arms. Soon afterwards, however, he had surrendered to the English a second time, and this time finally. From a brief imprisonment in the castle of which he had once been governor, William of Douglas had been moved to the Tower of London, and there about the end of 1298 he had died—or, as the Scots believed, been murdered.† His forfeited estates had been bestowed on Edward's adherents, Douglas itself on lord Clifford and the Northumbrian manor of Faudon on the earl of Angus; the English widow of his second marriage, James's stepmother, left penniless with two small sons, had been reduced to begging from Edward the restitution of her dower from her own first marriage; and James himself, orphaned and destitute, had found a home with Lamberton. It was probably Lamberton who had counselled the present approach to Edward. When redemption of their estates was being permitted to men who had fought the English for years, it cannot have seemed unreasonable to think that James, guiltless of any offence but being his father's son, might hope for a like grace.

* Complaint to Pope Clement V in 1306.
† In *The Bruce* Barbour states as a fact that William of Douglas was murdered. There is no evidence as to the manner of his death. Barbour's statement is, however, evidence of what the Scots—and, undoubtedly, William's son—believed in the matter.

He might not. As soon as he learned whose son this petitioner was, Edward's face began to darken. He had none but unfavourable memories of the late lord of Douglas. A violent, lawless man, William had first brought himself to the King of England's notice by abducting and forcibly marrying a well-dowered English widow, Eleanor de Ferrers, but this offence paled beside his later enormity in allying himself with Wallace. Wallace had rapidly become in English eyes a compendium of all savageries, 'a sacrilegious man, an incendiary and a homicide, more cruel than the cruelty of Herod and more insane than the fury of Nero' (*Flores Historiarum*), and that a nobleman should have associated himself with this outcast had profoundly shocked the perpetrators of the Berwick massacre. Edward wanted no son of Sir William's as his vassal. William, he declared, had been a traitor, his estates were justly forfeit, the loyal Clifford should not be deprived, and William of Douglas's son could look for nothing from the King of England. His notorious anger was beginning to rise, and Lamberton, the last man to dissipate his influence in openly pressing a hopeless case, hurried the boy away from the presence of the terrible old man. The Hammer of the Scots watched them go, unaware that he had just dismissed the future Hammerer of the English.

Chapter 1

The Disinherited

> The Fairy went up to the cradle and said:
> 'My poor child, the best thing I can give
> you is a little *misfortune*.'
>
> Thackeray

For James, Edward's rejection of his suit established that his sole hope of regaining his birthright lay in Scotland's casting off English rule. A frail hope it may have seemed at a time when the outcome of eight years' war, Wallace's near-success of 1297 and the long, weary struggle thereafter was seemingly total failure, but James was young and he could wait. He had already begun to learn patience in a harder school than that normally undergone by boys of his age and rank.

At his birth all had seemed set fair for him.* His father was head of a house of established wealth and nobility even though it was not among the score or so great families that then dominated Scotland, his mother was sister to the High Steward of Scotland (who, from their sharing a then rare Christian name, may have stood godfather to his nephew), and James was heir both to the Douglas barony and to the Northumbrian manor of Faudon with which, some twenty years earlier, his grandfather had augmented the Douglas estates. A privileged child, he seems also to have been a happy one until the outbreak of the war of independence

---

* The date of James's birth is not known, but it cannot have been later than 1288, at the end of which year his mother was dead and his father remarried, or much earlier than 1285, since in 1297 he was young enough to be called 'a little boy'. It has traditionally been ascribed to 1286, the year of Alexander's death.

and his father's engagement in it tore up the fabric of his childhood.

At the time William's last imprisonment began, James was

> a little knave,
> That then was but a little page,*

a reference indicating that he had by then taken his place in some noble household—possibly his father's, more probably another—where in the intervals of waiting on its head and on the ladies of the family he would receive, first as page and then as squire, the education deemed proper for a nobleman's son. There he would have learned to speak French (if indeed he had not done so already, for it was still the common tongue of the upper classes), and not only to speak, but to converse, for to be awkward or tongue-tied was a breach of good manners. He would have been taught to sing, if he had anything of a voice, and to play; he would have learned horse-management and received some preliminary instruction in handling arms; he would probably have been taught reading, less probably writing, for while he could have expected in adult life always to have at his disposal clerks to do the writing he would authenticate with his seal, he should be able to assure himself that they wrote only what he intended; and for the same reason there may have been instilled into him a smattering of Latin, still the language in which official documents, private as well as public, were couched.

From this mediaeval prep-school world James, still probably less than twelve years old, was at about the time of his father's first surrender switched to the slums of Paris. The object of his removal was perhaps to forestall his seizure as a hostage for Sir William's good behaviour;† its immediate result must have been as bewildering to a little boy as to any East End evacuee plunged into the deep country on the outbreak of the Second World War. Luckily for himself, James was a cheerful and resilient child. The little aristocrat settled down happily enough in this strange

---
* See Note on quotations, p. 172 below.
† William of Douglas surrendered to his parole, as unable to find the hostages he had promised. James, who would certainly have been an acceptable hostage, was apparently not offered, and the treatment the English accorded William (who was put in irons) would be consistent with their regarding his failure as wilful.

world, making friends among the city poor who were now his neighbours and getting into the mischief inevitable to an active boy left without occupation. In later life James thought his sojourn in Paris had served him well in teaching him how to get on with people of all sorts and conditions, and it may also have benefited him in another way. From the start of his active career James was to be notable, in a society where the conduct of war was still largely governed by convention, for military unorthodoxy, and this he may well have owed to passing the most impressionable years of adolescence among people to whom traditional upper-class codes of conduct were meaningless.

The news of his father's death and his own disinheritance shocked him out of his happy time-wasting. It is said, and his later conduct supports the tradition, that he vowed at this time to regain all that had been his father's,* but that this could be more than a dream he owed to Lamberton. It was the bishop who, having probably encountered James on his first embassy to Paris in 1299, gave the boy a home in his own household and, no less importantly, ensured for James a return to the conventional education without which he could scarcely hope to recover the station in life to which he had been born.

It is uncertain how far the training afforded well-born boys in those days was consciously designed to fit them for their likely adult functions. These could be taxing to a degree unparalleled today. In an age when professional specialization was all but unknown, the landowner might find himself called on to act by turns as policeman, lawyer, soldier, administrator and politician, demands that could be ignored only at the risk of losing the position that gave rise to them; James's generation would spectacularly illustrate the downfall possible, from the highest level of all, for one who neglected the duties while enjoying the privileges of rank. No man could govern the demands that might be made of him, and at their most exacting these could be met only by men who were mentally and physically both well endowed and well trained. Though it is certain that boys were drilled in the requirements of fighting, evidence of the intellectual education

---

* Almost certainly he made a vow of some kind. An acrostic on his name quoted in the *Scotichronicon*, so old that by the time it was recorded its second line had been lost, begins: 'Jure juventutis Jacobus jota justificatur'.

provided them is harder to come by, and it could be that this was largely left to a process of osmosis. The young squire would naturally attend his lord about the duties of adult life, and it may have been left to him to pick up in doing so the knowledge of law, of politics both local and national and of the management of men and of business that he would need to discharge the similar duties that would ultimately devolve on himself. With such a system of education the lazy and stupid would probably end scarcely less ignorant than they began; but quick-witted, intelligent boys could have benefited greatly, especially if they were lucky enough to serve an important and conscientious lord.

James could hardly have been better placed than with Lamberton. Mediaeval bishops exercised in their temporalities all the powers of great lay lords, and the secular training of boys entrusted to them would have matched that to be had in an earl's household. Lamberton himself was tireless in his care for his diocese, a man whose followers could never have been left in doubt of the responsibilities of rank. And beyond all this, and perhaps most important to the future of young James, Lamberton was throughout the years James spent with him at or near the centre of national affairs. Nor did his concern for Scotland lessen on her becoming an English fief. If James were privy to the bishop's thinking in the months that followed Edward's dismissal of his own suit, he would have known that there were clever and experienced adults for whom Scottish independence was not a lost cause.

When he paid homage to Edward, William Lamberton had bowed down in the house of Rimmon. The Scottish church had behind it a long tradition of independence of all authority but Rome's, and when Edward's advancement of his overlordship had threatened it with subjection to an English archbishopric the leaders of the church, chief among them Lamberton and bishop Wishart of Glasgow, had thrown their weight behind the national cause; nor had its apparently total failure quenched their hopes. Patient and persistent as Bruce's probably mythical spider, Lamberton was already beginning in the ruins of one insurrection to weave the fabric of the next.

One thing, it seems, he had already decided: the country's secular leadership must be changed. Balliol, his incompetence proved as king, was now contentedly settled in Picardy; his kinsmen the Comyns, who had directed Scottish affairs in his default, were incapable of ousting the English. Lamberton considered the alternative line. Old Bruce of Annandale, Balliol's rival for the crown,* was dead, but his claim survived in his grandson Robert Bruce, earl of Carrick, a man now thirty years old. Robert's record was not impressive. Notable for his tergiversations even in an age when national loyalty lacked the almost religious potency with which later ages would invest it and a change of allegiance entailed little stigma, Robert had at the start of the war adhered to King Edward rather than recognize his family's rival as King of Scots. That allegiance he had obeyed so far as to ravage Douglasdale in 1297, when Sir William was absent with Wallace, and abduct Douglas's wife and children, only to undergo immediately after—and perhaps from shock at his own actions—a revulsion of feeling that carried him to the Scottish insurgents with the declaration that he could not endure to be at strife with his own flesh and blood. For a short time he had even served as Guardian of Scotland with John Comyn of Badenoch (and, briefly, Lamberton) but the partnership between these quick-tempered and mutually hostile young men had not endured, and in 1302 Robert had returned to Edward, with whom his allegiance still ostensibly lay. An unpromising history, certainly, but Lamberton was not dependent on the record; he knew the man.

At Cambuskenneth Abbey on 11 June, a week before Stirling's fall and almost within sight of Edward's camp outside its walls, the earl of Carrick and the bishop of St Andrews met and entered into a treaty, under bond of £10,000 to be directed to war against the infidel, of mutual aid, consultation and defence against all other persons whatsoever. Such bonds were not uncommon in a day when central enforcement of law was unreliable and men looked for safety in association, but they normally included a saving of the duty owed the king. Lamberton's and Bruce's bond contained no saving, for any king.

Lamberton's sponsorship of an unwelcome protégé had not damaged his standing with Edward. The first manifestation of the trust the King of England placed in the bishop was the confiding

* Both had claimed by descent from David of Huntingdon, younger brother of William I of Scotland. Balliol, grandson of David's elder daughter, had claimed by seniority, Bruce, son of the second daughter, by nearness of blood.

to him of the Steward's eldest son Andrew—James's cousin—who had presumably been taken as a hostage for his father's good behaviour. Next, the bishop was named as one of the twelve Scots commissioners appointed to confer with the English on a future form of government for Scotland, in which capacity he attended Parliament at Westminster in the summer of 1305, to be added, during his stay in the south, to Edward's council for Scotland. At Westminster Lamberton could have seen and heard much to interest him: that English governmental finances were and for some years had been badly strained; that Edward's magnificent health was beginning—not surprisingly, since he was sixty-eight—to fail him; and that the Prince of Wales did not seem to have inherited much of his father's ability. These findings and their implications he may have discussed, on his return to Scotland, with the earl of Carrick.

The Westminster Parliament, twice prorogued, continued into September, and Lamberton and his suite may still have been there when on 22 August William Wallace, captured earlier that month, was brought to Westminster to stand his trial. Charged with treason, sedition, homicide, arson and a host of lesser crimes, Wallace declared he was no traitor for he was not and never had been King Edward's vassal; the rest he scornfully ignored. The verdict was never of course in doubt, and despite his just claim that he could not have committed treason it was to treason's punishment, of hanging, drawing and quartering, that he was condemned. The victim of this sentence, bound to a hurdle, was dragged through the streets to his gallows, there hanged, taken down still living, castrated and disembowelled. His head was then struck off and his body dismembered. This death Wallace underwent at Smithfield the same day. His head was placed on London Bridge and his body distributed in pieces about the country.

Edward's lieutenant for Scotland, John of Brittany, could not take up his duties until the spring of 1306, and in October 1305 Edward appointed four temporary Guardians until Lent. Lamberton was one of them, and it was probably this office that brought him, some time in the late winter, to Berwick to meet the council. Fronting the North Sea and swept by the bitterest winds of the compass, Berwick was a chill abode in winter and at any season now a bleak dwelling for Scotsmen. Ten years ago this had been the queen of Scottish towns, 'so populous and busy that it might well be called a second Alexandria';* now it was the epitome of defeat. Edward had driven out such native citizens as survived its capture, and planted an English colony there. English vessels thronged the harbour, English voices were heard in the streets, the castle was staffed with English troops and the town bound with walls raised by the English king, while the visible symbol of Scottish failure might be seen in the blackening, branch-like object nailed over the town gate: the right leg of William Wallace.

To Lamberton's carving-squire this colonized town must have represented a personal as well as a national grief. It was under his father Berwick had been lost. To Berwick Sir William had been brought in chains, and Berwick had been his last sight of Scotland when he was taken south to the Tower and his death. Of family as of national disaster James had a constant reminder. The southeast tower of Berwick Castle, once the Hog Tower, was now called—whether for the governor or the prisoner is not known— the Douglas Tower.

It was at the end of February or early in March that a messenger in the Bruce livery rode into Berwick with a letter to Lamberton. This letter, one of a number sent out to the magnates of Scotland, notified the bishop that Robert Bruce had proclaimed himself King of Scots; and that the declaration had been preceded by the killing of his principal rival for rule in the kingdom, John Comyn of Badenoch. Whether or not the letter mentioned the circumstances of the killing, Lamberton could have learned from the messenger the one fact now certainly known about it. It had taken place in the church of the Grey Friars at Dumfries, before the high altar.

Inevitably the English and the Scots chroniclers give different accounts of this murder. The English make it a premeditated and treacherous assassination, the Scots, however embarrassed by its location, an otherwise justifiable killing of a traitor who, having conspired with Bruce concerning a new rebellion, had then tried to betray him to Edward. That the act was premeditated is unlikely. Both Bruce and Comyn had uncommonly low flash-points, and if the former—who, both sides agree, had appointed the meeting— had approached Comyn with any intent of killing, he would certainly not have fixed a meeting-place where bloodshed meant sacrilege. The murder in itself increased the already tremendous

* *Lanercost Chronicle*, translated by Sir Herbert Maxwell.

difficulties of the enterprise he had undertaken; the sacrilege multiplied them.

This must have been very plain to Lamberton as, having had Bruce's letter read out to his household assembled at dinner, he sat considering its implications. When he had decided to back Bruce for the kingship, he must have realized that the change of leader would handicap Scotland both nationally and internationally. Balliol, hopelessly inadequate as he had proved, had been Scotland's crowned and accepted king, and efforts to restore him to his throne had had the justification of legitimacy. The substitution of a rival meant at the least yielding that strength, and from the Comyns—Balliol's kinsmen and, in the Badenoch line, next heirs to Balliol's claim—support for the Bruce would in any case have been doubtful. But in killing John Comyn Bruce had assured to himself the total enmity of this powerful clan and, there could be little doubt, had precipitated the civil war Scotland had suffered so much to avert. And in compounding murder with sacrilege he would almost certainly have incurred papal excommunication. For Lamberton this factor, with its threat that the clergy of Scotland might find themselves compelled to choose between loyalty to Bruce and to the universal church, may have been the most disquieting of all. Meditating the implications of Bruce's act, the bishop may well have wondered whether Scotland's best interests would be served by supporting his former ally. He was at least able to postpone his decision. Until he could get away from this English-garrisoned town, he would not be expected to declare himself. For the present he had only to temporize.

One member of his suite felt no hesitation. As soon as dinner was over James sought an interview with the bishop. Granted it, he came straight to the point. His heritage was in English hands, he could never hope to regain it unless the English were expelled, and the self-declared king was bound to attempt the expulsion. Would Lamberton approve his joining Bruce?

This request might appear to compel Lamberton towards an immediate commitment. To send his squire to Bruce would be a suspect act in English eyes, while to withhold this eager recruit—if he could, for James was not tractable—might be thought a sign of hostility by the man who held his bond for £10,000. Lamberton, however, was a practised resolver of seeming incompatibles.

James might go, with the bishop's blessing and with money for his journey, but he must appear to do so without consent. He might even take the bishop's palfrey for transport, but if the responsible groom objected he must do so against opposition. Ostensibly Lamberton must know nothing of his departure.*

Perfectly unconcerned at the prospect of leaving the household that so long had been his home with the reputation of a thief, James closed with the offer. The stigma entailed was in fact negligible, for theft by the well-born was apt to be judged in the light of its motive. No Scot had thought the worse of Simon Fraser for taking with him, when he changed sides from English to Scots, another man's horse and armour, neither was anyone whose opinion might matter to James likely to think the worse of him for apparently stealing Lamberton's palfrey and money to serve the national cause. Hurrying off, he collected his possessions and made for the stable, where he led out the horse—we are told his name, Ferrand, the iron-grey—and began to saddle him. As Lamberton had foreseen, the groom saw what was happening and tried to stop the boy. Taking the fullest advantage of the permission given him, James struck the man down, finished harnessing Ferrand, mounted and left. In the fading light of a late winter afternoon he rode out of Berwick and turned his horse westward to seek Robert Bruce.

* It has been suggested that this account was invented by James, to cover an actual theft. There is, however, no evidence that he was untruthful, except for military purposes, and the incentive for lying here was small. Further, the story was presumably known in Lamberton's lifetime—he predeceased James by two years only—and remained uncontradicted by him.

Chapter 2

The Disastrous Year

> His [Bruce's] mishaps, flights and dangers; hardships and weariness; hunger and thirst; watchings and fastings; nakedness and cold; snares and banishment; the seizing, imprisonment, downfall and slaughter of his near ones and, even more, dear ones (for all this he had to undergo, when overcome and routed at the beginning of his war) no one now living, I think, recollects or is equal to rehearsing all this.
>
> Fordun (*Cronica Gentis Scotorum*)

It is not known whether James had been at Douglas when Robert Bruce raided the barony early in 1297; the English chronicler, Walter of Guisborough, who alone recorded the episode saw no reason to number or name the 'parvuli' then carried off prisoner with Lady Douglas. The Scots understandably ignored the affair. For them the first meeting between the hero-friends of their historical epic took place, by the Arrick-stone at the head of Annandale, in March 1306, when James of Douglas met the newly proclaimed king riding north with his entourage to be crowned at Scone, offered his service and, accepted, did homage to Robert.

> And thus began their acquaintance,
> That never after any chance
> Could sever while they living were.
> Their friendship waxed aye mair and mair.

Not that either could have realized the significance this encounter would later hold for them. To James, certainly, the occasion may in itself have been momentous, for the performance of homage was one symbol of reaching manhood, while for him it may also have signified his formal setting-out on the recovery of Douglas that had long been his aim. To Robert, however, daily receiving new homages and reckoning up the power they represented, the tall, black-haired, lisping boy must have been among the least important of his noble recruits. Lacking money, lacking followers, lacking even the basic armament of a gentleman, with nothing to offer but his green and untried self, James cannot have appeared much of an accretion of strength. But Robert received the lad kindly, James fell in at his back in the procession to Scone, and the story began that would end in Spain a quarter of a century later.

On 25 March 1306, bishop Wishart of Glasgow placed the crown on the head of Robert Bruce, and even James, taking his place for the first time in an assembly of the nobles of Scotland, must have realized how incompletely attended the occasion was. The Comyns and their kindred were not the only absentees. Others not of that connection were lacking who had formerly played their part in the national effort, nor were these abstentions necessarily due to fear or apathy. It must have seemed highly doubtful still to the uncommitted whether their country's interests would be well served by upholding a usurper, a man whose previous service in the national cause had been devoid of notable achievement, and one whose assumption of power had been signalized by, on the most charitable reckoning, an act of political folly which could inspire little confidence in his future performance.

Of those who had thrown in their lot with Bruce's, James himself typified one group, the dispossessed who saw in the expulsion of the English their only hope of regaining what they held rightfully theirs. Another, including the most distinguished laymen there, comprised Robert's friends and relations. He was rich in both. Among the few earls present one, Malcolm of Lennox, was among his closest friends, a second, John of Atholl, was his brother-in-law by his first marriage, and Donald of Mar, a child, was his nephew and ward. His brothers alone made up an impressive group. There was Edward, next in age to the new-crowned king, a conceited, ambitious man but a doughty fighter; Thomas; Alexander, dean of Glasgow, remarkable for his brains —he had been the most brilliant student of his time at Cambridge; and Nigel, the youngest, remarkable for his beauty. With them were Christopher Seton, an English knight, Robert's brother-in-law and perhaps at this time his closest friend, and Thomas Randolph, his half-sister's son. Among so many promising young men the new-come James could have had little prospect for advancement. It is doubtful, in any case, whether he looked for it. He had not, after all, joined the new king to make a career but —as he had frankly told Robert—to regain his patrimony. His homage having been accepted, he knew that Douglas would be his if Robert ever controlled the barony, and his object now must be to do what he could to forward that situation.

Most notable, perhaps, of the witnesses of the coronation were the churchmen. These were men who had nothing to gain for themselves by upholding Bruce, and very much to lose. They included, besides Wishart, the abbot of Scone, David, bishop of Moray (uncle of Wallace's dead colleague Andrew Murray, and as devoted a patriot as his nephew) and Lamberton. Resolved at last to hold by his bond, the bishop of St Andrews had slipped out of Berwick under cover of night and hurried to Scone to lend his support to Bruce's hopes.

It was a makeshift ceremony. Robert's robes had been made in haste from ecclesiastical vestments supplied by Wishart, his crown knocked up by a local goldsmith. There was no bard to chant the new king's lineage, no earl of Fife to place him on the stone of coronation, indeed no stone. The earl, a minor, was in England in Edward's keeping, and so was the stone that with the other palladia of Scottish royalty had been carried south as a trophy of war. But one defect proved reparable. Two days after the coronation Fife's sister, the countess of Buchan, arrived at Scone. Her husband, head of the Comyns, was now at blood feud with Bruce, but devotion to her country—or, as the English chroniclers inevitably declared, her passion for Robert—overcame wifely loyalty, and she had hastened north to play the traditional part of the Macduffs in the coronation of a King of Scots. That she might do so the ceremony was repeated, and one part of the ancient ritual observed.

Before leaving for Scone Robert had garrisoned and victualled his own castles in the south-west, and as many as he might seize there of the English- and Comyn-held fortresses. Now he rapidly set about mastering as far as he might the rest of the country, and increasing the number of his homagers. The weeks after his coronation saw his powers reinforced by some distinguished recruits, among them Simon Fraser, perhaps the most famous Scottish soldier then living, and (an accession that must have been especially pleasing to young James of Douglas) James the Steward of Scotland. Not all recruitments were as voluntary as these. The earl of Strathearn, for instance, was kidnapped by Malcolm of Lennox and persuaded into doing homage to King Robert by the suggestion that if he persisted in refusing it his head should be cut off. Such an allegiance as this would obviously hold only as long as the threat remained enforceable; and the counter-threat was rapidly nearing.

Old King Edward's health might be failing, but on learning that the Scots were up in arms yet again he had set himself with undiminished will and a rage surpassing all that had gone before to mastering, finally and utterly, the ungrateful rejectors of his rule. His cousin Aymer de Valence, appointed his lieutenant in Scotland, was sent north to tackle the rebellion as speedily as he could; Edward himself and the Prince of Wales would follow with the full levy of England. Valence on his journey northward was followed by a fusillade of letters expressing Edward's fury, his vengeance, his demands—precise to the point of pedantry—for havoc to be wrought on the rebels in general, on the killers of Comyn, on specified individuals. Valence was to put to death all rebels already and hereafter taken, to burn, destroy and waste their houses, lands and goods. From the general Edward moved to the particular; one surviving letter requires Valence to burn the manor and destroy the land and goods and strip clean the gardens of Sir Michael Wemyss, and to do likewise 'and if possible worse' —Edward's wrath must have been outrunning his powers of expression—to the property of Sir Gilbert de la Hay; and Edward would make good the damage to the persons to whom he had granted the land. It was an extraordinarily, almost insanely, methodical rage that not merely provided for the king's carpet-biting to be carried out vicariously but undertook in advance to defray the cost of the carpet.

Moving rapidly northward, Valence gathered the English forces in southern Scotland, mustered the Scots hostile to Bruce and on Edward's command 'raised dragon'—unfurled the dragon banner that was an accepted token that the war to be waged would be, on the raiser's side, without quarter. The fourteenth century had no Geneva Convention, but there were nevertheless certain understood restraints that obtained unless a state of total war were proclaimed. It was such a war, hitherto unknown in the strife for Scottish independence, that Valence now declared against Bruce and his supporters.

Valence soon had good news for Edward. Early in June Wishart was captured in the castle of Coupar Fife, where he had taken charge of the defence, and a week later Lamberton followed him into captivity. The bishop of St Andrews had apparently ventured into negotiations with Valence, trusting perhaps to his honey tongue to extricate him from any danger. He swore his innocence of complicity in Comyn's murder, and produced excuses for his attendance at the coronation and his delivery to Robert of the boy Andrew Stewart, but when a copy of his 1304 bond with Bruce came into the hands of the English he was in a snare from which no eloquence could free him, and soon was on his way south, in chains, with Wishart. Only their cloth saved them from Wallace's fate; theirs was imprisonment, one in Winchester, the other in Porchester Castle. Edward was greatly rejoiced by these captures and wrote to Valence, now at Perth, that only Bruce's—for which he waited impatiently—could please him more. Valence's aim now must be to bring Robert speedily to book.

Robert himself was eager to come to grips with Valence. Nothing could do more to swing the waverers to his side than a speedy victory. Summoning almost all the forces at his command, he raised his standard in June and advanced to Perth for the confrontation. Somewhere in the army at his back, leading his first troops, assigned him by Robert (probably in recognition of his rank rather than of any potential he had yet shown), wearing his first coat of mail, provided by Robert, rode James of Douglas, ready for his first battle.

They came before Perth early on 18 June, and halted without the walls, drawn up in battle order, to await the English. No sortie followed. Valence, summoned by Robert's herald to do war, piously replied that the day was Sunday and hence ill-suited to any such undertaking; on the morrow he would be pleased to join battle. Robert, devout for all the hot-tempered sacrilege at Dumfries, accepted the declaration at its face value and withdrew his army to Methven some five miles distant. There, spreading about the wooded slopes, they began to make ready for night, watering horses, raising shelters, wandering off to forage for food, while knights shed their emblazoned surcoats for plain tunics of white linen or even discarded their armour wholly to bask in the warmth of the westering sun. In this pleasantly unbuttoned state Valence, marching forth at vespers to reap the harvest of his cunning, found the army he had to overcome.

Methven was not just a defeat, it was a rout. Relaxed and unready, the Scots had no time to form into battle order, many indeed no chance to arm and mount, before their enemies were on them. Robert managed to get to horse, have his banner unfurled and rally those nearest him, but it was a hopeless effort. He himself was all but taken, saved only by the unblazoned tunic that obscured his identity to the extent that his would-be captor, who knew him by sight, could not attract help before Christopher Seton struck him down. There was nothing for it but flight. Robert managed to disengage that small part of his force, some five hundred men, that had got and held together near him and withdrew with it to the hills where the English on their heavy horses could not pursue, but before night fell all the rest of the army that had marched so hopefully to Perth was scattered, prisoner or dead. James was one of the lucky ones who got clear of the field and with Robert fled for the hills. All his life after he was to show a concern with picketing that by the standards of his time bordered on the obsessive, and that may well have had its origin in his first experience of battle.

For a while they lurked in the hills, 'dreeing in the Mount their pain'; then, as Valence made no move northward, ventured to Aberdeen. There Nigel Bruce joined his brother, bringing with him Robert's wife, his daughter Marjorie, the countess of Buchan and other ladies of Bruce's party. For a little while they rested at Aberdeen, and then word came that Valence was again on the move. Robert dared not meet him, for the disaster at Methven had terribly diminished his shaky prestige:

> All the commons went him fro,
> That for their lives were full fain
> To pass to the English peace again.

He determined to go westward, to the wild country the English could hardly penetrate, where he might gather reinforcements to fight them again. His little army took horse and set out for the hills once more. It included, besides Robert's brothers, the earl of Atholl, Sir Gilbert de la Hay, Sir Neil Campbell, Sir Robert Boyd, and the unimportant James. With them went the ladies, for the state of all that party was that of outlaws, and even their women were in danger anywhere but in reach of the tiny army. Turning south, they plunged into the stony, inhospitable, stream-riven steeps of the Grampians, and soon were far from human habitation. In that harsh and empty world they were as dependent on themselves as if they had been on a desert island. Such a situation, as J. M. Barrie observed, is apt to expose the natural commander, and so it did here. That painful trek across the mountains and morasses of Atholl, peeling away the claims of birth, wealth and office, revealed unmistakably the two men destined to steer Scotland to her independence: Robert Bruce and James of Douglas.

It is through the events of this unhappy summer that Robert Bruce, aged thirty-two, can first be seen as a man not only ambitious but fit to rule. His previous record, distinguished if at all chiefly for vacillation and blunder, gives little hint of the king and general he was to prove. He may have been a very late developer; unquestionably capable of learning from his mistakes, he was all his later life to show himself remarkable for growth in wisdom and capacity. It may be, too, that his powers were of the kind that are most fully tempered under stress. If adversity was for him a maturing factor, he had it in plenty now. His situation was dreadful. Having ventured everything, he had lost almost at once the greater part of his resources, while his present condition, as uncomfortable as it was dangerous, was shared by others many of whom were dear to him and all his responsibility, who had been brought to this plight by his ambition and his failure. For many of them, as certainly for him, the fate of Wallace was very near. Yet whatever his inward dismay he gave no sign of it, remaining outwardly good-tempered, hopeful and buoyant. It is not, however, surprising that he now began to be more and more drawn to the one person in that company who, while recognizing their danger, was unperturbed, who was always ingenious in mitigating their hardships and who without false optimism remained genuinely cheerful.

This was James. He was flourishing, and no wonder. Day-long riding through rough country in all weathers, trapping supper and eating it charred from a camp fire, sleeping mail-clad on the ground or watching by night for the approach of enemies are not at twenty the hardships they may be at forty. Bouncing with energy and hardy as a wildcat, James thrived on the privations that were wearing down his seniors. Even the tribulations of his childhood were now paying dividends; long inured to the dispossession his companions faced for the first time, he can scarcely have had time to think that he was farther than ever from Douglas when every day brought new experiences and new enterprises, the satisfaction of achievement and the additional satisfaction of knowing it observed. He had even—rare indulgence in war—the eyes of ladies in which to shine. He may in fact have been running a love affair at this time; he certainly managed to create the impression that his hunting, a pursuit surely enjoyable in itself for a lad his age, was all done for the sake of the ladies.

It was seemingly by this hunting that he first attracted attention. In that flight through barren country all depended for food on what could be killed. Hunting, of course, was then the principal pleasure of the noble, and most of the gentry present must have been expert in the great chases and drives that swept whole countrysides with hound and horn. But even had the terrain allowed them, such self-advertising methods were not for men themselves the quarry of men. What they needed now were the arts of the poacher, and in these James rapidly showed himself proficient.

> For whiles he venison them brought,
> And with his hands whiles he wrought
> Gins to take pike and salmons,
> Trouts, eels and eke minouns [minnows] . . .
> There was not one among them there
> That to the ladies' profit was
> More than James of Douglas.

Early in August they reached the springs of Tay, and struck out westward. They were now approaching Macdowel territory. The Macdowels of Argyll and Lorne had formerly been active in the national interest, but Alexander of Argyll had been husband to John Comyn's aunt, and the Dumfries killing had swung him and his to the English side. Alexander was an old man now, but his powers were wielded by his son John of Lorne, and John was bent on avenging his cousin. At Dalry near Tyndrum on 11 August he and his caterans fell upon Bruce's little force. Man for man Bruce's mailed warriors would have had no difficulty in overcoming the lightly weaponed and unarmoured Highlanders, but they were greatly outnumbered and the Argyllmen, two or three to one and shrewdly attacking the horses, soon began to overwhelm them. Robert saw that once again there was no hope but in retreat and, disengaging his men, covered their withdrawal himself with a magnificent rearguard defence. Many bleeding—among them James, who had received his first battle wound from one of the Highlanders—and many afoot, they got away, and the second encounter of the reign ended in the second defeat.

This setback, coming on top of the sufferings of the journey, engendered a despondence that even Robert's determined cheerfulness could not overcome. The women were exhausted, as indeed were some of the men. The earl of Atholl, older than most of his companions and worn out by what he had gone through, said plainly that he could go no farther. Better to return eastward, where at least they could rely on shelter and food, than to continue the gruelling struggle through country no less infested by enemies than the eastern counties. Robert, unlike most kings and indeed many noblemen of his day, was always prepared to consider the views of others and probably realized moreover that the obligatory continuance of the unwilling could only weaken such morale as remained in the rest. He yielded to Atholl so far as to divide his forces. Atholl, with Nigel Bruce, Robert Boyd and the women, would turn back, taking some half of the troops, and go to Kildrummy Castle in Aberdeenshire, one of the few castles Robert held in that district; there they would almost certainly undergo siege, but Kildrummy was strong enough and sufficiently provisioned to hold out until winter compelled the raising of sieges. The rest would continue westward with Robert in search of reinforcement. He was heading now for Kintyre, where he had friends among the Macdonalds and where Dunaverty Castle offered a base from which he could summon the Islesmen, but the Macdowels barred the overland route there and Kintyre would have to be approached by sea. Neil Campbell, who had kinsmen in that district, went ahead to try and secure ships, and the rest, turning southward to avoid Macdowel country, set wearily off to follow him to the coast.

James, whose injury cannot have been a serious one, remained with the king's troop. It could hardly be called an army now; two hundred men on foot—the surviving horses had been assigned to the Kildrummy party—plodding the rough tracks of Balquhidder in filthy clothes under rusting mail, their feet cased in the coverings of hide they had cobbled up from skins when their shoes wore out. Before them lay, they hoped, the comfort of Dunaverty, but there was still much land and water to cross before they got there, and the very first obstacle brought them up short. They came to Loch Lomondside, and found no ferry to cross.

This was disquieting, for a detour round the loch would not only delay but endanger. Northward lay the vengeful Macdowels, southward the Lennox. Lennox had once been friendly country, but nothing had been seen or heard of earl Malcolm since Methven, no one knew what his earldom now might hold, and the castle of Dumbarton, strongly garrisoned by the English, lay only five miles from the loch's southern tip. The shore was desperately searched until James, scouring the water's edge, found 'a little sunken boat' and pulled it in. It was a mere skiff, with room for only two besides the oarsman, but it was all they had and it had to do. Robert crossed first, taking James with him; then the boat returned, and so to and fro for a night and a day until all the two hundred were on the western shore. While they waited there for the ferrying to be completed Robert told the story of Ferumbras, and how Charlemagne's Twelve Peers were shut up in a tower and besieged by vast hordes of Saracens, yet were relieved and came to good ending. He enjoyed the popular romances of the day, and had a great stock of stories taken from them; he had of late been drawing much on those that told of people who faced and passed apparently overwhelming odds.

Before setting off again Robert divided his troops into two, thinking the smaller groups could more easily forage for their needs, and sent the second off with James. Making their way safely to the rendezvous with Campbell, they rejoined the king and found with him, unexpected and most welcome, the earl of Lennox and some of his people, encountered by Robert and his party as they trudged to the coast. The general joy of the meeting was reinforced by Campbell's achievement in securing provisions as well as the needed ships, and the whole troop was soon more cheerful than for many days. But the English were near, and no time could be lost in embarking for Dunaverty. Nor could any muscle-power be spared from the oars. Everybody, however unskilfully, set to:

> And fists that stalwart were, and square,
> And wont to span great spears were,
> So spanned oars, that men might see
> Full oft the hide left on the tree.

Lennox, who delayed in embarking, all but fell captive to some of the men of his own earldom, and escaped only by jettisoning his baggage to lighten and speed his ship. Dunaverty was safely reached, but Robert dared not linger in a refuge so obvious now his movements were again known.* Again they took to the galleys, heading first for the little island of Rathlin off the Irish coast; thence into obscurity.

Robert's whereabouts from September 1306 until the following January are one of the minor enigmas of Scottish history. Barbour believed, possibly because the trail ends and starts again at Rathlin, that he and the three hundred men now with him spent the whole period on this small island inhabited by peasants living at the subsistence level; the English chronicler Guisborough, that he was in 'the farther isles'; the later Fabyan, that he went to Norway, from which it has been conjectured that he was in Orkney, then Norwegian territory; while the Macdonalds of Loch Duich preserve a tradition that at this time he visited their castle of Eilean Donan. Wherever he went he was, as later events show, at some time in touch with Ireland, while some intermittent contact may have been made with the Scottish mainland. According to Guisborough he sent to Carrick at Michaelmas for his rents, and at some time during the months of obscurity his force was rejoined by Sir Robert Boyd.

Boyd, who in 1305 had been the English-appointed coroner of Clydesdale, had nevertheless been one of Bruce's earliest and most active supporters, having in March 1306 seized Rothesay Castle for the new king and followed up the capture with a vigorous attempt on Inverkip.† He had been one of the Kildrummy party,

---

* Dunaverty was in fact under siege by 22 September.
† He had also been associated with Lennox in kidnapping the earl of Strathearn; it was Boyd who proposed the beheading of that nobleman unless he did homage to Robert.

and now he brought the evil news that Kildrummy, fired from within by treachery, had fallen and its defenders been taken by the English. He himself had later escaped; Nigel Bruce had not. The one piece of comfort Boyd could have offered would have been that Robert's wife and daughter, with Atholl and the other ladies, had got safely clear of Kildrummy before the castle fell.

Robert was now planning an early descent on the mainland. Delay until summer would enable Edward to gather a force far outnumbering any he could muster, and at a time when warfare was largely seasonal a winter invasion might bring him the advantage of surprise. His assault was to be two-pronged, he himself landing from Arran in his own earldom of Carrick with his brother Edward and most of the Scots, while his younger brothers Thomas and Alexander, with a force recruited in Ireland, made a diversionary descent on Galloway. For the movement to Arran, Rathlin was to be the gathering point, and there towards the end of January Robert's force began to assemble.

The feeding of these incomers inevitably bore hard upon the peasants of Rathlin. James of Douglas, either genuinely perturbed by this or seizing on a possible excuse for more activity, suggested to Boyd that rather than add to the burden on these poor folk they might precede the rest to Arran and try to provision their troops there. Boyd, who knew Arran well, agreed; they obtained Robert's permission and set off in the one galley that sufficed to take their combined following, probably no more than three dozen men, so scanty now were the forces of independence.

Coasting Kintyre, they reached Arran at nightfall and landed near Brodick. The galley having been dragged ashore and hidden, they set off towards Brodick Castle, now occupied by the English lord Hastings, on whom Edward had conferred the Isles with the earldom of Menteith. Luck was with them, for they chanced to reach Arran the same evening as did the deputy warden of Brodick Castle bringing three ships loaded with supplies for the castle and arriving too late to permit unloading before night. Under cover of night Boyd and Douglas concealed themselves with their men between the castle and the slipways, and waited there till next morning. Then, when Hastings' men had unloaded the stores and were carrying them up, they burst from their ambush, scattered the unprepared English, drove back into the castle the guards who had rushed out to tackle them and—the men still by the boats having put to sea with such panicked haste that two of the vessels capsized—seized their spoil, food, wine, armour, all they could want, and carried it off. Moving into the remoter parts of the island, they took possession of a wooded glen which if need be they could hold against any troop Hastings might dispatch in search of them, and there dwelt for nine days, till on the tenth the sound of a familiar horn summoned them out to their reunion with Robert.

Prepared though he now was for descent on the mainland, Robert had no intention of committing himself blindly to action. A scout, one Cuthbert, was sent to Carrick with instructions to sound out the people there, weigh the situation, and if he found it propitious light a signal fire on the coast towards Arran. Watch was kept, the fire sighted and the small army crossed to Carrick, there to be met by a half-distraught Cuthbert declaring that the fire was not of his lighting and that he never would have lit it. The omens were as bad as they could be. Carrick was swarming with Englishmen, Turnberry alone was occupied by a force under Henry Percy which equalled Robert's whole army, and the tenantry, utterly cowed, dared not raise a finger for their earl.

To refrain from action was one thing, to withdraw from it another. Having once begun, Robert resolved to go on, and to act at once. Marshalling the newly landed troops, he led them straight to Turnberry, where they burnt the sleeping town, slew all the Englishmen they could find and took up position before the castle. There they remained three days, until word of their coming penetrated to Ayr, a relieving English force set out for Turnberry, and Robert withdrew into the Galloway hills. By that time he had heard from his kinswoman, Christiana of the Isles, what had befallen his kindred and friends. It was nothing but evil.

Nigel Bruce was dead. He had been hanged at Berwick in October.

Christopher Seton was dead. Taken by the English when Lochdon Castle was surrendered by its keeper, he had been hanged, drawn and beheaded at Dumfries.

The women had been captured. Escaping as far as Tain, they had been seized in St Duthac's sanctuary there by the earl of Ross and handed over to Edward. His knightly conscience forbade the execution of ladies, but his old ingenuity in devising punishment had not deserted him, and for the countess of Buchan and

Robert's sister Mary he had invented a treatment that shocked his own son. These two young women had been imprisoned like wild animals in cages, with egress only to privies, one in Berwick Castle and one in Roxburgh. The twelve-year-old Marjorie, Robert's only legitimate child, his wife Elizabeth and his sister Christian were prisoners in England.

Simon Fraser was dead. Captured the previous summer, he had been taken to London and there hanged, drawn and quartered. His head stood now on London Bridge beside the decaying mask of Wallace.

Above them rotted the head of Atholl. Trying to escape from the north-east by sea, he had been captured by an English galley, taken to London and there hanged on gallows built thirty feet high in salutation to his Plantagenet blood. The ailing Edward was said to have benefited greatly from the report of his execution.

To the named dead there were joined scores of Scotsmen, knights, commons, even priests; every adherent of Robert's who fell into Edward's hands he had executed. Those who survived were those who had abjured, abandoning in despair a leader who could neither hold on to what he had nor protect his followers.

Nor was this the nadir. Robert can scarcely have withdrawn from Turnberry when news reached him of the landing in Galloway. It had met immediate and total catastrophe. On 10 February Dougal Macdowel had encountered, defeated and captured Thomas and Alexander Bruce, and one week later they were executed in Carlisle.

A venture unpromising from the first had shrunk to a ghastly farce. The freedom fighters of Scotland were now a few score men skulking on the fringe of an occupied country, their base an empty range of hills, their armament what they could carry on their backs, their transport their feet. Their kin and allies were a scatter of decaying bones on half a dozen town walls, their living friends terrorized into passivity, and their destruction was the prime object of a great nation and of an active and powerful minority among their own compatriots. For many of Robert's followers it must have been little beyond despair that held them with him. Where surrender could offer no hope of life, fealty might as well be served; they were doomed anyway. But there were some who even at this juncture might reasonably have hoped to save their necks by yielding, and James was one of these.

Innocent both of complicity in Comyn's murder and of oath-breaking to Edward, he could not be charged with either of the offences that meant certain execution, while his youth and, to the English, his unimportance could in themselves have been arguments for mercy. Had he sent to offer surrender, and he must have known Scots now on the English side who would have acted as intermediaries for him,* he might well have obtained a promise of life and perhaps even of liberty.

James was in fact at this time weighing up his personal situation, but it was not safety that was uppermost in his mind. What was irking him was the thought that a year had passed since he left Lamberton with the expressed intention of redeeming Douglas, and all that while Clifford had enjoyed undisturbed possession of the barony. James could tolerate it no longer. His home now was little more than fifty miles distant, and there he determined to go while he could, to make it plain to Clifford that Douglas was no rightful property of his. Coaxing an unhappy assent from Robert, who not surprisingly had begun to dread partings, he set out, taking with him only two troopers.

> That was a simple staff to take
> A town or castle for to win.

James believed he could do it.

* His Gallovidian cousin, Bernard Cathe, or Keith, was one of these; at about this time he lent Valence 73 marks.

Chapter 3

Douglas Regained

> I like a lord of mettle,
> Who mailed and mounted leads
> His followers to battle;
> Who's foremost in the fighting,
> In cut and thrust delighting,
> His valour them inciting
> To match with theirs his deeds.
>
> Bertrand de Born

Descending into Douglasdale with his two companions on an evening in mid-March, James halted a little outside the village and sent a message to the farm of Hazelside asking its tenant for a meeting. This man, Thomas Dickson, whom James remembered from childhood as a valuable servant of his father's, was among the wealthiest and most influential of the Douglas tenants, and seemed both in himself and in his local importance the man most likely to be of help in any enterprise against the English. James had chosen well. On seeing his dead lord's son Dickson cried for joy, and eagerly entered into his plans. He smuggled the three men into Hazelside, produced the best food the farm could offer, and set out to sound the likeliest supporters of a possible rising against Clifford's men. Those who seemed sympathetic were introduced into Hazelside one by one—nothing must be done to arouse the suspicions of the occupying English—and gathered in the chamber where James awaited them. There he told them of his hopes.

It did not seem odd to these men that a lad some twenty years old, a stranger to all of them since his childhood, should appear from nowhere and ask them to risk their necks in an almost ruined cause. The functional division of society was still generally accepted even by those on whom it bore hardest, and leadership in war and politics was the function of the knightly class. The young man was literally doing what he was made for. James, moreover, had already the gift of infusing others with his own confidence, and any misgivings about the enterprise itself quickly dissolved in the warmth of his enthusiasm. One by one, Dickson the first, the Douglasdalers knelt and did homage to the vital young campaigner as their true lord.

The formalities over, James got down to business. Asking for all they could tell him about the disposition of the English forces, the state of things at the castle, the numbers of the garrison there and their habits, he learned that on important feast-days the captain of the castle normally led the entire garrison, some thirty strong, to mass in the parish church of St Bride. It was now Thursday, 16 March; the coming Sunday was Palm Sunday, and unless they had some cause for disquiet the English soldiers would certainly be there. James resolved to seize his chance and take them in the church, reflecting perhaps that his novice warriors would probably do better in an enclosed place than in the open. The thought of launching a battle in church apparently caused him no qualms; he cannot have been among those who attributed to the consecrated ground of Comyn's murder the subsequent misfortunes of his killer. Perhaps he felt that St Bride—his family's chosen saint, by whom he himself literally swore—would understand and aid him.

Sunday came, and with perfect confidence the captain of Douglas Castle marched his men out to mass. He had, after all, no cause for alarm. The last embers of Scottish resistance were flickering to extinction fifty miles away, an English army lay between him and them, and Douglasdale itself seemed no less resigned to English lordship than at any time in the past eight years. The garrison marched out, palm in hand, and down to St Bride's, and word of their going was carried to James, loitering inconspicuously near the village with a peasant's mantle shrouding his mail. It had been agreed that he and his two professionals should not be in church with the Douglasdalers when the service began, lest the sight of strangers alert the English; his entry was to be the signal for attack. He in his turn set off with his troopers for the church and, climbing the knoll on which it stood, heard shouting within and the clash of weapons, and knew their plans had gone awry.

What had happened was that one of the Douglas men, his nerves perhaps overwrought with the strain of waiting, had suddenly given the cry of 'Douglas!' and rushed at the English. Dickson had joined him, the rest of the Douglasdalers, startled and confused, had hesitated. The Englishmen, though without their armour and taken by surprise, had their swords with them, and they were professionals. The two Scots were promptly struck down, and the English captain hurriedly formed up his men in battle order in the chancel. It was at this point that James burst in, saw what had happened and realized that his only hope lay in instant renewal of the fight. Shouting to the Douglasdalers to follow, he flew at the ordered English ranks, and a moment later the men of Douglas, rallied less by his call than by his example, came on at his back. This time there was no faltering. Soon the English were all either dead or prisoners, and the lord of Douglas was marching triumphantly towards his castle. Half a dozen men went ahead to take possession; the porter and the cook, who alone remained in the castle, were easily secured; and James entered the fortress of his ancestors.

There was no question of holding it. News of his action would be abroad in a day, and the English could detach men and armaments enough to overwhelm him without any perceptible reduction in the forces gathering against Bruce. But for the moment he could preside in his own hall. The cook, when captured, had just finished preparing dinner for the garrison, and James and his men sat down and enjoyed it. Having dined, they scoured the castle for everything worth taking away; money, weapons, clothing were baled and loaded for removal. This done, James launched them on an orgy of destruction that, however exhilarating after the strain of the last few days, had behind it the cold purpose of leaving nothing to the English that could possibly be of use. The castle stores were ransacked and its provisions, too bulky to carry off, dragged into the cellar. Sacks were ripped open, meal and malt and grain strewn about the floor, and barrels staved in to porridge them with wine. Salt was thrown down the well, and dead horses after it. Finally James had the prisoners brought into the ravaged cellar and beheaded. Then, leaving their headless bodies sprawled in the mess of food and wine that earned the whole affair the name of the 'Douglas Larder', he fired the castle and with his men vanished from Douglasdale. Militarily, he had scarcely dinted the vast structure of English power. Psychologically he had pulled off a coup to disturb the sleep of every English garrison in the country.

In later centuries James was to be much blamed for his 'barbaric' action in killing his prisoners. Significantly, no such criticisms were made by the chroniclers, Scots or English, near to him in time. Even where no symbolic declaration had been made of total war, the killing of prisoners, and particularly of captured garrisons, was not unusual; on the fall of Caerlaverock in 1300 Edward I had hanged a number of the garrison, and a like fate would befall the garrison of Cumbernauld at the hands of Edward Balliol in 1335. The Douglas Larder, moreover, fell in a period of total war, proclaimed not by the Scots but by the English, who, as shown by the fate of Thomas and Alexander Bruce, were still fighting under the sign of the dragon displayed the previous year. The enemy he fought had set James no precedents for mercy.

Even so, it is doubtful if any thought of vengeance was in his mind when he ordered the prisoners killed. Though he could be ruthless where ruthlessness brought advantage, he was seldom governed by impulse even in youth, and nothing in his career suggests vindictiveness. Almost certainly there was reason behind these killings. What none of his critics has suggested is an alternative compatible with his duty to his own people. He could not keep his prisoners in custody because he had nowhere to hold them; they certainly could not be kept in the scattered hideouts to which he was now taking his own men. But the only other course open to him, to set the surviving Englishmen free on his departure from Douglas, would have risked the lives of the followers for whom he was responsible. A resistance leader in heavily occupied territory, he was sharply conscious of the dangers that surrounded him and them.

> So dreaded he Englishmen's might
> That he durst not well come in sight.

Only twenty-five miles down river lay the fortress of Bothwell, with sixty men-at-arms in its garrison. Release of any of his prisoners would have ensured the arrival within twenty-four hours of a punitive expedition guided by Englishmen who knew the environs of Douglas and the likely places of concealment there. James himself could have got safely clear before its arrival, but several of his own men besides Dickson had been hurt in the fighting and could not travel far. These men he moved first to the nearer hideouts, contriving to get leeches to attend to their wounds,* while he himself with the uninjured men lurked in more distant concealments until he could safely lead the whole troop into Galloway.

News of Robert was not lacking. He was still uncaptured, every added day he was at large quickening his country's almost extinguished hopes. So did the reports of his achievements. Tales were running through the land: how alone he had slain three men suborned to murder him; how he had held a ford single-handed against two hundred; how Valence, advancing with a large force into Glentrool where the English thought Bruce unsuspectingly bottled up, had been knocked head over heels by Robert and his men cascading down the glen sword in hand. After weeks of beating the Galloway hills with the troops of northern England and the anglophile Scots, Valence was no nearer running down his quarry, and the numbers he would have to deal with were growing. The great host old Edward was assembling at Carlisle no longer seemed a sledgehammer to break a nut already gripped by the crackers, for 'notwithstanding the terrible vengeance inflicted upon the Scots who adhered to the party of the aforesaid Robert de Bruce, the numbers of those willing to establish him in the realm increased from day to day' (*Lanercost Chronicle*). James, returning to Robert with many more men than he had taken away, rejoined a force likewise augmented, and probably enlarged his own troop yet further with a share of the new recruits. Many of these must have come not with any feudal lord but singly or in small groups, needing a divisional leader to whom they might attach themselves. Those who were Lowlanders, probably the majority, would naturally prefer a Lowland captain, and many must have been attracted to the young Lowlander who had brought off the Douglas Larder. Certainly the Douglasdale contingent alone is unlikely to account for the increase in his personal following from the little

---

* Dickson apparently survived, for Robert subsequently granted Symington in Lanarkshire to 'Thomas filius Richardi' whose descendants still held it, with Hazelside, in the seventeenth century.

group of January—for whom, with Boyd's, one galley had sufficed —to the sixty-odd men he had at his back by May.

Part of his increased human resources he invested in scouting. Having grasped more thoroughly than most men of his time the value of good intelligence, especially to the outnumbered, he was already

>James of Douglas, that all tide
>Had spies out on ilka side.*

It was not long before his 'spies' proved their worth. News came to him that Valence, disturbed by the increasing disaffection in Kyle, was sending a large troop under Sir John Mowbray to reinforce the English there. Either learning or deducing the road Mowbray would take, James moved to intercept him near Kilmarnock, choosing a position at a ford called Edryford. This was approached by a track over marshland so boggy that horses could safely move only on the path itself, while on the farther side of the ford the ground rose abruptly with the path narrowing to ascend it. Behind this rise James and his sixty men awaited the enemy. All night they lay there, and in the morning saw across the marshes a line of approaching horses with Mowbray in the van. Holding fire until the leaders were actually in the ford and the following troops waiting to cross, they then sprang up and loosed a flight of arrows on the unsuspecting men.

Lined up along the path, the English could neither deploy to counter-attack nor turn to fly without bogging their horses. The safest course for them was in fact forward, to drive right through the attacking foot-soldiers. Only Mowbray, however, saw this, and when he spurred his horse up the path none followed. He burst through, leaving his sword and broken belt in the hands of a Scot who had made a valiant effort to pull him out of the saddle, and galloped for Inverkip Castle—where his swordless and unattended arrival created great surprise—while the Kyle reinforcements struggled in the morass or fled back the way they had come.

Encounters like that at Edryford, however miniscule their effect on his total strength, exasperated Valence. The Scots could be met in arms only where they were not expected, while every en-

---

* Barbour thrice applies this couplet or a variant of it to Douglas, and uses it of no other captain.

deavour to bring them deliberately to battle found them elusive as smoke. When, rarely, he managed to get his main force near Bruce's assembled army, it simply ceased to exist as such, dissolving in small groups impossible to pursue and re-forming again in another district entirely. An attempt to match this gambit by using a bloodhound to track down Robert among his scattering troops narrowly failed, and ended unpleasantly for some of Valence's men when the Scots, regrouping faster than had been thought possible, beat up that night an unguarded English camp that had been noted by James as he led his men to the reassembly point. Constant failure to dispose of so insignificant an enemy, besides ensuring a succession of wrathful letters from old Edward, was affecting the morale of Valence's own captains; his inquest on the Glentrool affair had ended with Clifford and Vaux at fisticuffs. Deciding to try and goad his adversary into battle, he sent a direct challenge to Bruce, whom he invited to meet him honourably in open battle rather than continue 'skulking'. This provoked at any rate the answer Valence wanted. Robert sent an answer declaring he would meet Valence with his army by Loudon Hill on 10 May, and gathered in his forces for the encounter. He had, however, no intention of granting Valence another Methven, and 9 May found him already at Loudon Hill, studying the ground.

The road under the slope of the hill, on which he expected to meet Valence, ran over firm ground which offered a wide field for troops to manoeuvre, but to either side, about a bowshot from the road, lay morasses as boggy as that into which Douglas had driven Mowbray's men. Robert had now six hundred fighting men at his back, besides the servants and 'small folk' who might help in a pursuit but could not be expected to stand a charge, but he knew Valence would bring far more against him, many of them heavy cavalry. He determined to narrow the front on which he must meet them. On either side, inward from the marshland toward the road, ditches were dug, deep and wide enough to halt the advance of cavalry, until the gap between them was no wider than five hundred men could ride through abreast. Behind the first pair of ditches a second was dug, and then a third. Early on 10 May Robert sent off his 'small folk' to await the issue behind him on the hill, and formed up his men-at-arms across the gap between the first two ditches, in a position that could not be outflanked, with a double line of defence in reserve behind, to meet an enemy funnelled against their spear-points. All went as he had planned. Valence, keeping his appointment with three thousand men, found them facing a line of spears, unassailable in flank or at the rear, that repulsed every frontal attack. Repeated assaults brought only increase of losses till the survivors of the vanguard, which alone he had been able to bring into play, lost heart and began to retreat, so dismaying the yet unengaged rear as to start off a flight in which he had no choice but to join.

Robert, elated by victory, followed up his triumph with a march to Ayr, where he laid siege to the castle, but in this he over-reached himself. The disproportion in numbers was still so great that the defeat even of three thousand little diminished the resources employed against him, and the attack on Ayr simply told the English where to concentrate next. At the approach of a relieving army he withdrew again to the hills.

The English had, all the same, undergone a grievous humiliation, that chafed to fury the old man at Carlisle. The king, wrote an unidentifiable member of his entourage to a likewise unknown correspondent in London, was much enraged that the Guardian (Valence) and his forces had retreated before 'King Hob'. The writer went on to give the latest news from the north; David of Atholl—son of him whose head was decaying on London Bridge—had come to the king's peace; James of Douglas had sent and begged to be received, but drew back on seeing the king's forces retreat; there were rumours of treasonable dealing between some of the English and the enemy. Rumours evidently filled the air, for the writer ends by saying that what was heard one day was contradicted the next.

The statement about James was probably a rumour alone; had he ever considered a change of sides the time would have been in February or early March, when Robert's fortunes were at their lowest—and at that time James had resoundingly demonstrated his allegiance by setting off to perpetrate the Douglas Larder—rather than when they were plucking up, in May. James, moreover, had played a conspicuous part at Loudon Hill, an unlikely action if just previously he had been trying to secure acceptance with the English. If there was anything more in the story than baseless gossip, the explanation may lie in the reference to 'treasonable dealings', and James's concern with getting information. If there had indeed been some fraternization, he may well have taken advantage of it to try and pick up news of English movements—many of the Scots now with the English in Galloway, who included his cousin Bernard Cathe and Thomas Randolph, must have been known to him—and he may have created an impression, deliberately or otherwise, that he was wavering in his fealty. But only one firm conclusion as to James can be drawn from that letter: he was now of sufficient interest to the English for the news that he had thought of changing his allegiance to be worth reporting to London.

For all his triumph, Robert had begun to consider a fundamental change in strategy. The Scots' inferiority to the English in wealth and population was a fact of nature; they would always be outnumbered and out-munitioned by their enemy, and to try and drive that enemy out by confrontation in battle was too dangerous a gamble. A defeated English army would be replaced, a defeated Scottish one might be irreplaceable. The alternative was to make Scotland too costly to hold, and this was the course on which he now determined. English armies should not be faced in the field, but left to march about till frustration and the cost of maintaining them led to withdrawal. English detachments and English garrisons should be unnerved by guerrilla warfare and picked off one by one as opportunity arose. Castles regained from the English should not be retained, pinning down scarce Scottish troops to be eventually overwhelmed by superior numbers and armament, but demolished, never again to terrorize the Scottish countryside under the control of invaders. This was the strategy of which the more dramatic aspects were later cherished in popular remembrance and be-rhymed as the great king's legacy to his successors.

> On foot should be all Scottish war,
> By hill and moss themselves to steer.
> Let woods for walls be bow and spear,
> That enemies do them not dare.
> In strait places gar keep all store,
> And burn the plainland them before,
> Then shall they pass away in haste
> When that they find nothing but waste.
> With wiles and wakening of the night,
> And mickle noise made on height,

> Them shall ye turn with great affray
> As they were chased by swords away.
> This is the counsel and intent
> Of Good King Robert's Testament.

Though popular remembrance linked these techniques with Robert's name alone, it is likely that James had much to do with their framing and adoption. The Douglas Larder, undertaken when Robert was still waging war, as far as he could, on traditional lines, embodied all the principles of the new strategy right down to the attempt to destroy Douglas Castle. James had been the first, as he would always be the most consistent and successful, exponent of the new policy.

At some time during the summer he returned to Douglas.* Clifford on learning of the Larder had hurried to his ravaged holding, where he restored the castle—the stonework of which had of course survived the fire—replaced the garrison and installed one Thirlwall as captain before returning to Valence. Hearing of this, James had arranged for various alarms to be raised about the castle by way of testing Thirlwall's readiness to emerge and deal with them and, finding the response satisfactory, made ready to exploit it. Moving overnight to Sandilands, about five miles downstream from Douglas Castle, he took up a concealed position with most of his men, and in the morning sent a small detachment to the castle as cattle raiders. After a while the cattle pounded past with James's men driving them on, and behind them, stringing out along the valley in pursuit with the armoured but helmetless Thirlwall at their head, came the English. Shouting, the Scots burst from cover. The Englishmen, scattered as they were, could make no effective defence. Thirlwall, standing to fight with those he could rally, was killed, and the remaining men fled for the castle with the Scots in full cry after them. A few got back. The rest were cut down, many in full view of the castle walls, the gates were slammed and barred, and James, who had no intention of wasting men in a fruitless attack, departed once more, having

---

* Barbour places the second attack at Douglas, as he does all incidents of this summer, before Loudon Hill, even suggesting that James, most improbably, spent the entire time between the Douglas Larder and this attack in hiding near Douglas. Barbour's sequence of events here is, however, suspect; he may have been unconsciously moved by the wish to make the victory at Loudon Hill the climax of the summer campaign.

served clear notice that Englishmen could expect no quiet in Douglas as long as he was at large.

With the continuing discomfitures of the English, above all with the plain and indisputable victory of Loudon Hill, Scotsmen all over the country were plucking up heart and polishing their weapons against the day when Robert should approach and summon them to action. Five days after Loudon Hill an unidentified Scot on the English side wrote from Forfar*:

> I hear that Robert de Bruce never had the goodwill of his own followers or of the people generally so much with him as now. It appears that God is with him, for he has destroyed King Edward's power both among English and Scots. . . . I fully believe that if Bruce can get away in this direction, or towards the parts of Ross, he will find the people all ready at his will more entirely than ever, unless King Edward can send more troops; for there are many people living loyally in his peace so long as the English are in power. May it please God to prolong King Edward's life, for men say openly that when he is gone the victory will go to Bruce.

It did not please God. On 7 July Scotland's deadliest enemy died at Burgh-on-Sands, his last aggrandisement incomplete.

By the end of July Edward II had reached Carlisle and taken command of the army assembled by his father for the fourth and final conquest of Scotland. On 2 August it crossed the Border at last. On the 6th it was at Dumfries, on the 18th at Sanquhar and on the 26th at Cumnock where James the Steward—who had abjured Robert the previous autumn—entered into a bond of 500 marks for his good behaviour. On 26 August the English army struck camp, and turned towards England again. Early in September Edward marched it over the border once more, dispersed it and left for the south, taking Valence with him and leaving another cousin, John of Brittany, as Guardian in his stead. As far as he was concerned, the reconquest of Scotland could wait.

As Edward broke up his army, Robert reassembled his. In September he swept into Galloway (*CDS*, vol. iii), 'burning and

---

* Translation by G. W. S. Barrow (in *Robert Bruce and the Community of the Realm of Scotland*) of a letter printed in *Calendar of Documents Relating to Scotland* (*CDS*), vol. ii.

plundering and ravaging and inciting and compelling the inhabitants to rebel'. Some districts he ravaged so fiercely that the peasants fled, driving their herds before them, into Cumberland for safety, while from others he took tribute as the price of leaving them in peace. But though he could terrorize he could not yet subdue Balliol's resentful lordship, laced as it was with hostile fortresses. The whole country of the Lowlands was indeed too firmly held by the English and by anglophile Scots to offer a secure base for the recovery of Scotland and Robert's thoughts were turning to the north. There English resources were thinly spread, with great tracts of wild, ungarrisoned country islanding the castles and walled towns they held, and there the strenuously independent men of Moray, inflamed by their bishop's preaching, were only awaiting his coming to rise in arms. There too waited the earl of Buchan, head of the Comyns and leader of the anti-Bruce forces among the Scots, who must be dealt with before Robert could begin to think himself truly King of Scotland. Towards the end of September or at the beginning of October he left for the north, taking with him his brother Edward, the earl of Lennox, and indeed his entire following except for James and his personal troops. They were left, sole representatives in the Lowlands of Robert's sovereignty, to consolidate and if possible extend his holding there.

James made at once for Douglas. Despite the recent mortality at the castle Clifford had managed to replace the second garrison and to instal in Thirlwall's place as captain a knight called John of Webbiton, a fierce young man given to flaunting himself about Douglasdale, whose readiness to venture out of the castle needed no testing. James decided that a variant of Thirlwall's end should do for him. Accordingly one morning the watch on the castle walls saw a troop of peasants leading down the valley packhorses laden with bulging sacks, and reasonably concluded that grain was being taken to Lanark fair for sale. Webbiton heard of this with great satisfaction, for in Douglas Castle—as no doubt in all the southwestern outposts after Edward II's pointless parading of his great army—supplies were low, and here was a chance to replenish them at no cost. Summoning his men, he armed and spurred out in pursuit, and soon was overhauling the pack-train. But the yokels leading it, far from displaying a decent alarm, promptly flung off their mantles, whipped out swords, cut loose the sacks (which were in fact stuffed out with grass) and, springing to the horses' backs, faced round upon their pursuers. At this the English, now perhaps remembering Thirlwall, checked and turned back towards the castle, only to see James and another troop breaking from ambush behind them. Too shaken to combine in defence, unable to escape the closing pincers, they were quickly and completely dealt with. The Scots, investigating the dead Webbiton's purse, found there an explanation of his acceptance of his dangerous post; a letter in a female hand coyly indicating that when for a year he had held the castle of Douglas, 'that to keep so perilous was', he might indeed hold himself worthy of a lady's favour.

The English tenure of Douglas was at an end. Those that were left of the garrison yielded the castle. James let them go unharmed, even giving them journey-money, and took possession. With no fear now of immediate reprisal, he had the castle totally demolished in compliance with now approved strategy and as the best insurance that Clifford, who would never try to hold this dangerous valley without walls to shield his men, would not attempt to repossess Douglasdale. Then, leaving his barony as secure as he could hope to render it in these insecure times, he turned eastward and passed into the Forest.

At this time the hills and valleys of the central Lowlands were still clothed in the remnants of the ancient Caledonian Forest. Bearing no likeness to the man-made coniferous forests of present-day Scotland, this was a vast, little-inhabited tract of deciduous woodland, oak and birch and thorn mingling with alder and willow in the swampy valleys, that swathed the country from Peebles-shire to the English border. The roads of Lowland Scotland skirted its fringes, the paths that wound into its depths being little known or used save by the foresters. Royal charters identified three separate forests, of Ettrick, Selkirk and Jedburgh, but to Lowland Scots the whole sweep of wooded country was simply *the* Forest.

Control of the Forest was now an obvious goal for James. West of Douglasdale lay Carrick, already returned to Robert's sovereignty, northward the territory in which the Steward—time-serving with the English, but covertly sympathetic—was dominant lord, while Galloway to the south, bristling with English-held fortresses and bitterly hostile to Bruce, was more than James and his little troop could tackle. The Forest, moreover, had attractions of its own. Its trackless depths, penetrable only by those who knew it well or had the foresters' trust, made it an admirable base for guerrilla warfare. Wallace had so used it, as had Simon Fraser. The English, indeed, recognizing its dangers, had once attempted to seal it off with a ring of strongholds, a task akin to hedging in the cuckoo, for those who held the Forest could within it move from point to point on its periphery faster than any force seeking to control them from outside. James already knew something of the district, for one of the principal residences of the bishop of St Andrews lay at Stobo in its north-west range, and he must have realized that here was the perfect theatre for his kind of war.

The parts nearest Douglasdale also now represented something of a power vacuum. The northern Forest had until 1304 been dominated by the Frasers of Oliver Castle, whose line had ended with Simon and whose forfeited lands had been granted to Valence, thus leaving, as far as native authority was concerned, a gap James might fill. Could he do so, he would also secure a valuable recruiting-ground. According to Walter of Guisborough the men of Ettrick were notable for their fine physique, 'well-made men of great height', and were reckoned the best archers in Scotland. At Falkirk they had distinguished themselves by their stubborn heroism, fighting and falling where they stood under the leadership of the Steward's younger brother, John of Bonkle, who at the last had dismounted to die fighting on foot among them.

His nephew now found an eager welcome among their sons. Within two months James had so far swayed the Forest to Robert's allegiance that John of Brittany found it advisable to take possession of Valence's fortresses in Selkirk and Teviotdale in the hope of getting Selkirk Forest again under control. He was wasting his time. The Forest might be hemmed in with hostile keeps, but for James it was now itself a stronghold three counties wide.

Busy about his new dominion, he was spared, till it was over, the worst alarm yet to shake the nationalists. Robert, advancing towards Buchan to try conclusions with its earl, had within reach of the opposing army fallen suddenly and seriously ill. For a while, as his troops lay encamped about his sickbed and his archers skirmished daily with Buchan's, his survival was in doubt. Buchan, however, did not venture to attack even when, the king fit at last to be moved, his army set slowly off with weapons at the ready to carry him to Inverurie. He was convalescing there when, just before Christmas, David of Brechin, one of several nobles of Angus who had brought support to Buchan, attacked his outposts and killed several men. This defiance so enraged Robert that despite his weakness he insisted on mounting his horse and leading out his men in a challenge that dismayed Buchan and his allies into almost immediate flight. The battle of Inverurie opened the gateway to Buchan and on this province, the centre of Comyn power, Robert now loosed an assault that was probably intended to teach all his opponents in Scotland that he was no less to be feared than the English. The remaining Comyn strongholds were seized, sacked and demolished, and the whole district given over to a ravaging so complete that fifty years later it was still remembered and mourned as the Herschip, the harrowing, of Buchan. With Moray friendly and Buchan totally conquered, Robert had a secure base in the north, and could spare men for the Lowlands once more. Early in the summer of 1308 Edward Bruce came south again, accompanied by Robert Boyd and Alexander Lindsay, to invade Galloway, and Douglas emerged from the Forest to join them.

Edward Bruce may already have received from his brother the former Balliol title of lord of Galloway, which he was using the following year. If so the grant was in the nature of an incentive, for Galloway could be secured only by conquest. A part of what had once been Cymric country, later successively ruled by Northumbria, by Strathclyde and by the Hebridean Norse, Galloway had been subsumed in Scotia only in the twelfth century, and the two centuries since had done nothing to instil in the Gallovidians any sense of identity with the rest of the kingdom. They preserved their own laws, their loyalty focussed on the hereditary lord of Galloway, John Balliol, and long Gallovidian memories still recalled that the earl of Carrick descended from a cadet of Galloway who had killed his brother, their lord. Edward could thus expect to face a triple resentment, as a Bruce, as Balliol's ouster, and as the representative of an unloved central authority. He made no attempt to conciliate the inconcilable, but entered as an invader 'and in one day slew many of the gentry of Galloway, and made all that district subject to him' (*Lanercost Chronicle*). Douglas accompanied him in that first savage raid, and may have been present when, towards the end of June, Edward fought and overcame near Buittle an English army under John de St John and the former Guardian of Scotland, Ingram Umfraville. But very soon after, and though all the fortresses of Galloway were still in hostile hands, he was in the Forest once more.

This separation may reflect a joint decision that the nationalist forces in the south could effect more apart than combined, but it may have resulted from friction. Edward Bruce outranked Douglas socially and hence, by the universal practice of the day, militarily as well. After his months of autonomy Douglas may not have enjoyed subordination to a commander who, albeit a dashing soldier, combined with stupidity a conceit so invulnerable that even his brother sometimes found it difficult to co-operate with him. In Edward Bruce's own opinion of himself, he was quite as fit as his brother to be a king, if not indeed more so; he did not, for instance, share what he doubtless regarded as Robert's foolish weakness for listening to, and sometimes even heeding, the views of others. He was the last man to pay attention to the notions of a raw youth who had hardly worn armour two years, the more so as these must have differed radically from his own ideas.

Edward Bruce and Douglas polarized contemporary attitudes to war. Douglas fought to win. Of all the commanders to serve in the Scottish War of Independence he was the most cautious; though possessed of the personal daring essential to war-leaders, he disliked hazarding his men's lives in doubtful ventures, and sought always to redress the numerical inferiority normal with the Scots with some countervailing advantage, preferably of surprise. Such circumspection was quite alien to Edward Bruce. Prey to the vanity whose achievements must be recognizably those of personal prowess, he wholly subscribed to the chivalric code which dictated that he whose enemy sought a fight should respond, openly and scorning advantage, to the challenge. The roots of this code went far deeper than the epoch of mounted warfare from which it took its name; the heroic legends of Ireland acclaim warriors who to fight a one-armed enemy would tie one hand behind their backs, while in historic times the Anglo-Saxon ealdorman Byrhtnoth, holding an invading Danish army at disadvantage beyond a river, acceded to their request that he let them cross and fight him on equal terms.* Edward Bruce would probably have ap-

* At Maldon in 991. Byrhtnoth, most of his army and numerous inhabitants of the district he was supposed to be defending paid with their lives for his chivalry.

plauded that decision; Douglas, who rated the confounding of the enemy above his personal reputation, later found himself in a situation almost exactly paralleling Byrhtnoth's and responded very differently. Ironically, it was not Edward but Douglas who was to be remembered by later ages as a paragon of chivalry.

Whatever his reasons, Douglas returned to the Forest, probably in July, and thence began probing into Lothian. This province, the most fertile in Scotland and the richest, was the most totally subject to the occupying power. The powerful fortresses of Edinburgh and Roxburgh nailed down two of Lothian's three corners, Berwick the third, and between them, along the best roads in Scotland, a string of lesser forts and peels reinforced their hold. Strengthening it too was the district's greatest lord, the earl of March, who almost alone among the native magnates had since 1296 consistently adhered to the English side. Militarily March might be worth little (Edward I had once sarcastically quoted at him: 'When the war was over, Audegier drew his sword'), but his support did much to aid the grip of the English on Lothian.* So did geography. The Lothian landowners had at their backs no wild country like the Lennox or Moray from which to harry occupying forces in their land. For them, adherence to Bruce meant abandoning their estates and their tenantry—and with these much of the aid they could bring him—until he could take the province from outside, and hold it. It would for them, in 1308, have been a grave gamble.

Douglas could not, of course, seriously menace this great redoubt of English power, but from the Forest he could at least remind the Lothianers, by raid and ambush, that there was another power in Scotland. He soon had made himself such a nuisance that Adam of Gordon, one of the principal barons of the district, decided that something must be done to stop him. Calling out his men and summoning two other Lothian knights to his aid, Gordon set off into Tweed-dale, Douglas's present haunt, to swat the gadfly.

There stood then in the valley of the Lyne Water, which joins the Tweed some three miles west of Peebles, a building large enough to shelter a considerable number of men, and on this one evening the two parties unwittingly converged. The Lothianers

* March died this year, but his son and successor followed the same policy and was equally inactive militarily.

reached it first, took possession and made themselves comfortable within; despite the errand that had brought them, they apparently placed no pickets. Shortly afterwards, Douglas approached with his usual caution. He saw that the building was already occupied, glided to the window to listen and find out by whom and, having soon heard enough to convince him that those within were no friends of his, brought up his men to the building and 'umbeset it all about'. The sound of movement alerting the Lothianers inside, they leapt to arms and burst out to tackle him. Gordon with most of his men broke the cordon and got away, but his companions were not so lucky and Douglas, inspecting his haul when the fighting was over, found he had netted two valuable fish. One of them, 'wounded in a place or two', was his own cousin, Alexander Stewart of Bonkle, son of that John Stewart who had died at Falkirk. The other was Robert's nephew, Thomas Randolph.

Of all Robert's kin who lived to play a part in public life, this nephew of the half blood seems to have resembled him most. His qualities were his uncle's on a lesser scale; as a general, as a diplomat, eventually as ruler of Scotland, he would later show himself worthy of every responsibility assigned him. But at this time he seems to have been—like Robert at the same age—a young man in a muddle. Despite Balliol connections on his father's side, he had joined Robert immediately on the murder of Comyn. Captured at Methven but spared at Gordon's plea, he had changed sides, probably as a condition of survival, and had rationalized his decision to such an extent that the previous summer he had been active on the English side in Galloway. Permitted to retain his manor of Stichill in Berwickshire, he had married a sister of Alexander Stewart, and by now presumably regarded himself as one with the anglophile group in Lothian.

Realizing at once that these were prisoners too important to be kept to himself, Douglas decided to take them to Robert and, hoping to win them to the national side, showed them all the consideration he might. He failed, however, to charm them into complaisance. Alexander Stewart, who, unlike his cousin, had not suffered forfeiture for his father's patriotism, had grown up in the English allegiance and was not going to change it overnight. As for Randolph, he must have been feeling very sore. Fully as lustful for glory as the average young knight of his time, he had so far distinguished himself in the great war chiefly by getting captured by each side in turn, the second time by what, sharing as he did his uncle Edward's views on knightly conduct, he probably regarded as a mean trick. Nor can it have sweetened him to reflect that his second captor was a young man who had started behind him in the race and now was pulling ahead.* His temper did not improve on the journey north. Received by his uncle with a friendly offer to let bygones be bygones, he retorted that the person whose conduct needed overlooking was Robert, who was behaving like a brigand instead of waging open and honourable war like a gentleman; whereupon the king had him placed 'in firm keeping' to cool off and think things over at leisure. Alexander Stewart apparently ransomed himself, for in 1310 he was free, and still on the English side.

Douglas's resolve to deliver his captives in person may have been partly influenced by the knowledge that Robert was planning a campaign against Argyll and by the hope of a chance to participate. Robert was breaking the sticks one by one. From Buchan he had moved his army to the borders of Ross. The earl of Ross, apparently less a Comynite than a fence-sitter who had come down on the English side when Bruce's cause seemed ruined, had mobilized in a defensive rather than an aggressive spirit and, impressed perhaps by the Herschip of Buchan, proved ready to enter into a short truce. Leaving him to utilize this in writing to Edward II for reinforcement, Robert marched towards Argyll with a force strong enough to alarm John of Lorne also into accepting a temporary armistice and in his turn sending to Edward for help. Ross may meanwhile have been reflecting that Robert was a great deal nearer than Edward and in much more of a fighting mood, for it does not appear that on the expiry of his truce he made any move to re-open hostilities, and in October he was to make total submission to Robert. But no like complaisance could be expected from the Macdowels, and by August Robert was preparing for a final reckoning with them.

The landward route into western Argyll, the main seat of Macdowel power, lay through the Pass of Brander. Here Loch Awe stretches its eastward arm that narrows and falls to become the

* The date of Randolph's birth is unknown, but he was probably rather older than Douglas; he had been a witness to Balliol's homage to Edward I in 1292. He was already a knight when captured at Methven.

River Awe on its way to Loch Etive and the sea. On either side the hills plunge to the water, Creag an Aonaidh on the south with almost precipitous steepness, the lower slopes of Cruachan scarcely less abruptly to the north. Even today the road must squeeze between water and hillside, and in the fourteenth century the track through the pass was so narrow that in places men could traverse it only in single file. Robert either had warning that John of Lorne planned to ambush him there or calculated that so obvious an advantage would never be ignored. Determined to surprise any would-be surprisers, he divided his force into two parts and assigned one to Douglas with the task of taking any ambush in the rear. The job was one wholly to Douglas's taste. Leading his division across the shoulder of Cruachan, possibly under cover of night, he located the Argyll troop, stalked them to their position above the pass, and moved his own force unperceived to take the height behind them. Looking down the hillside they could see the track far below, and to the left the waters of Loch Awe where galleys hung on their oars, one of them bearing John of Lorne who, kept probably by ill-health from leading his men on Cruachan, had stationed himself there to see his enemy swept into the loch. From the eastern end of the pass Robert's Highlanders came filing along the narrow track, and the heather sprang to life with Argyllmen yelling as they loosed a fusillade of bolts and stones on the men at the water's edge. But the Highlanders knew what to expect. Lightly armed and nimble, they were not to be daunted by any hill, and turned at once to scramble towards their assailants. Then, as the Argyllmen started downwards in a rush,

> Came James of Douglas and his rout
> And shot upon them with a shout.

The Argyllmen, readied for battle in the confidence that surprise was on their side, were utterly demoralized by this turning of the tables. As the Highlanders sprang up the slope from below and Douglas and his company plunged sword in hand from above, they panicked, broke, and fled westward down the pass to the one bridge across the Awe, their pursuers so hot on their heels that they had no time to break it before Robert's men too were across. The door to Argyll had been successfully forced.

Marching to Dunstaffnage Castle, the centre of Macdowel

authority, Robert besieged and captured it. This castle he did not demolish, but placed there his own garrison, well provisioned with the victuals he had commandeered from the surrounding country, and turned triumphantly back. The Argyll campaign marked the effective ending of the civil war. Though a number of Scots, including a few magnates, still opposed Robert and still were ready to do so in arms, they were henceforth to do so as auxiliaries of the English. None now was both able and willing to wage war in his own right. Buchan and Lorne fled to England, Buchan to die within the year, Lorne to maintain the fight in Edward's pay, sometimes very effectively,* until in 1316 he too retired, broken in health, to London to die, having sacrificed all he had in his fruitless efforts to avenge his cousin.

Robert was becoming king in fact as well as in name; the dissentients in Scotland now were less those who acknowledged than those who opposed him. How far he had come was made plain when at St Andrews in March 1309 he held his first parliament. This, if it could not yet be called representative, was still a very different assembly from the little group that had gathered to see him crowned. The ranks of the lords spiritual had been reinforced by the bishops of Dunkeld, Dunblane, Ross and Brechin; and again, astonishingly, included Lamberton. The previous year that remarkable prelate had contrived, even from his prison in Winchester Castle, to beguile Edward or those who had influence with him into permitting his release provided he remained within the bounds of Northamptonshire. Three months later he had secured his enlargement as far as the diocese of Durham. There only the Tweed lay between him and Scotland, and the final step, for Lamberton, must have been a mere nothing. At the parliament of 1309 his name was enrolled among those of Scotland's clergy who set forward their declaration that Scotland was an independent kingdom and that her king, true heir to Alexander III, was Robert Bruce. A like declaration was issued by the laymen. Those who placed their names to it included, besides the earls of Lennox, Ross and Sutherland, representatives of the communities of the earldoms of Fife, Menteith, Mar, Buchan and Caithness, whose earls were (except for Buchan) prisoners or minors; the barons of Argyll and the Isles; James the Steward, who was to die this year

* He managed to recapture Man a year after Robert's seizure of the island in 1313.

but had lived long enough to see the start of Scotland's recovery from the troubles he had endured with her; Randolph, now reconciled—for ever, it would prove—with his uncle; Robert Keith, Marischal of Scotland, the first Lothian landowner but already not the only one to gamble his heritage on Robert's eventual triumph; all the survivors of the little band that had held by Robert through the darkness of 1306, and among them, taking his place with the barons by right of possession no less than of title, James, lord of Douglas.*

* In all surviving documents he issued or attested James is described thus, showing that, though generally known to history as James Douglas, he had in fact no surname; Douglas was his territorial name only.

Chapter 4

The Fortresses Fall

> Good Sir James of Douglas,
> Who wise, strong and worthy was,
> Was ne'er o'erglad for no winning
> Nor yet o'ersad for no tining [losing],
> Good fortune and ill chance
> He weighed in one balance.
>
> Anon.

As a destitute and orphaned boy in a foreign country James had formulated his aim in life; to redeem his heritage. Within ten years he had virtually achieved it. Save for the minor English property, Faudon, he was now possessed of all that had belonged to his forbears, and could if he liked settle down to live as other barons lived, running his estates, playing his part in Lanarkshire affairs, perhaps discharging local offices, seldom concerning himself with matters of state but when summoned to parliament, and burnishing his armour only if disorder approached his home or the king called out the feudal host. It is doubtful if this possibility even occurred to him. Somewhere along the line means and end had changed places; taking up arms to recover Douglas he had discovered his calling in life, and Douglas repossessed was to be the home base of a professional soldier.

James of Douglas was one of those happy people who are born to a time, place and milieu that exactly suit their natural talents. Inventive and practical, his love of action directed by a shrewd intelligence and a genius for getting the most out of scanty resources, he might have been made to serve the needs of a poor, beleaguered, mediaeval country. These made no less demand on body than on mind and character, and this too he was perfectly fitted to meet. He was built for battle; a tall, broad-shouldered man, well made, muscular and lithe, his splendid body powered with health as splendid. He resembled Hector, declared Barbour, who like all western Europeans of the time believed himself descended from the Trojans and reckoned Hector one of the three greatest champions of ancient times.

Though not handsome—at least in the eyes of contemporaries, for whom his black hair and sallow skin were incompatible with beauty—Douglas had great charm. Terrifying on the battlefield, he was away from it quiet and even gentle in manner.

'When he was blithe, he was lovely', wrote Barbour, using the word in its old sense of lovable,

> And meek and sweet in company,
> But who in battle might him see
> All-other countenance had he.

Even the lisp with which he incongruously spoke was held in him attractive. This engaging personality must greatly have facilitated the advancement his abilities demanded. Personal factors weighed heavily in the public life of the day. Among noblemen, whose upbringing had generally inculcated in them more sense of their own importance than of the value of self-control, personal offence, easily given and easily taken, could dominate political conduct; the baronial opposition to the Crown in England at this time was greatly inflamed by the sheer bad manners of Edward II and Piers Gaveston. Scope for the able to offend was much widened by the customary mediaeval equation of executive authority with social rank, whereby the subordination of the highly born to men of lower birth could prove a potent source of rancour. But Douglas, who almost throughout his adult life exercised authority incommensurate with his rank, his age or both, seems never to have made a personal enemy.

> He bore himself in such manner
> That all him loved who were him near.

Certainly his own people did, and with reason. He cherished his men, gave his own share of battle spoils to be divided among them, praised them when they had done well, cared for their welfare; the sole surviving glimpse of Douglas at home shows him planning a feast for his men. Not surprisingly, he was rewarded with a first-class fighting force.

> He treated them so wisely aye
> And with so mickle love also,
> And such a countenance would make
> Of their deeds, that the most coward
> Stouter he made than a leopard;
> With cherishing thusgat made he
> His men strong, and of great bounty [excellence].

Douglas was certainly astute enough to observe that good treatment promoted efficiency, but it is not likely that anything but genuine goodness of nature would have moved the love he inspired, or left memories so cherished that when he had been a generation dead Barbour, mining the recollections of men who had known him, would find there the materials for the glowing portrait in *The Bruce*.

The nature of Douglas's following probably varied with the enterprise in hand. Its nucleus must always have been his own standing force of professional soldiers. This was small; he had no taste for conspicuous consumption, and would probably have laughed at those later Douglases whose dignity required even in time of peace the maintenance of a thousand men. He himself kept some two hundred under arms, the majority archers, probably drawn from Ettrick, the rest men-at-arms. It was no doubt these last, a troop some fifty or sixty strong, that he used for the small-scale, carefully planned guerrilla operations in which he specialized. They were tough and versatile men, ready as necessary to take their place with the twelve-foot Scottish spear in the close-packed ranks of a schiltrom,* to tackle their enemies on horseback with lance or axe, to scale a fortress wall by night, or unobtrusively to reconnoitre enemy movements in the scouting operations on which Douglas so much relied. These troops would be reinforced as necessary by those of Douglas's vassals—whose numbers would increase with his land-holdings—and the ranks of the professionals, at times when some exceptional effort was impending, by the local levies. These able-bodied men were required by a later

---

* Shield-troop, a name given to any close formation of soldiers on foot; a term surviving from the day when such a troop was remarkable chiefly for the continuous wall of shields it presented.

decree of Robert's to maintain a degree of military equipment related to their wealth (every man worth £10 a good sufficient acton, a bascinet and gloves of plate with a spear and a sword, and every man having in goods the value of a cow a spear or a bow with twenty-four arrows) and to turn out to use it when national need demanded.

Besides the resources of his own fiefs, Douglas was probably able when he needed to extend his strength to draw increasingly on those of the eastern and central Lowlands. It was usual in Scotland at this time for the lesser gentry—many of them, though tenants in chief, no wealthier than English country knights—to attach themselves to some greater lord whose standard they would follow in time of war. As March Warden later in his career, Douglas would in any case have been able to call on the services of knights who were not his feudal dependants, but it is likely that the tendency of the lesser landowners of the south and south-east to range themselves under his standard had its origin in the years before Bannockburn when the men of these districts, ready to fight for Robert but lacking among their own magnates any leader on the national side, were drawn there by the rising fame of the young Lowland commander.

By 1309 the process of prising loose the English hold on Scotland was under way. It had already begun while Robert was stamping out the last organized military opposition among the Scots. Sir Thomas Gray in his *Scalacronica* recounts two anecdotes of the previous year concerning his father, Edward II's castellan in Coupar Fife Castle, who on his way back from Edward's coronation was ambushed by, but got away from, Walter Bickerton, and who another time, hearing an affray raised in a neighbouring hamlet on market day and riding out to tackle it before any of his own people were ready, found the street filled with Alexander Fraser's troops out to capture him and fought his way back to the castle alone. The elder Sir Thomas was clearly a father to be proud of, but it is plain from the episodes cherished by his son that even in 1308 the English castellans north of the Forth ventured at their peril into the countryside they were supposed to be overawing, and Coupar Fife Castle was in fact in Scottish hands by 1309. In August of that year Edward actually issued a commission to Richard de Burgh, earl of Ulster and Robert's father-in-law, to treat with Robert respecting peace. This was the first of what were to prove many abortive negotiations, the ineffectiveness of which probably derived from the fact that the only term on which Robert was prepared to make peace was the only term to which Edward would not assent—English recognition of Scottish independence. A truce on the borders was, however, negotiated at the end of the year and, extended, ran till the next summer. Its expiry was followed by the reappearance in Scotland of an English army led by its king.

The English failure for the past three years to make any move in the upholding of Edward's claim—or to aid those Scots and English who were trying to uphold it on the spot—derived from Edward's preoccupation with what seemed to him a matter of more moment: the strife with his magnates which, originating in their efforts to secure a hold on government, had now come to centre on their determination to rid England of his hated darling, Gaveston. When in 1310 Edward at last came northward, bringing with him the lover he dared as little as he wished to leave behind, he was probably moved hardly less by his desire to get away from the opposition in the south than by the prospect of reconquering Scotland. Entering by the western marches in September, he advanced to Biggar, thence to Linlithgow and so, circling the Forest on the north, into Lothian and south again as far as Berwick. The Scots, pursuing Robert's strategy of withdrawal, melted away as he advanced—'not daring to meet them', as the English indignantly put it—only to advance as he withdrew, entering Lothian as Edward reached Berwick, to waste the lands of his adherents there in mocking demonstration of the worth of his protection.

Though the English campaigned only in the summer, winter warfare being impossible to their cavalry-oriented minds by reason of the dearth of grass for their horses, Edward wintered at Berwick and in the spring of 1311 sent the earls of Gloucester and Surrey marching through the Forest to receive the foresters to his peace. Douglas was probably not far away—the Forest was his favourite haunt,* and the English could never find him there unless he chose to be found—but he did not interfere; the foresters would be at his service when he needed them. He

* It may by now have belonged to him; at a date unknown, which could have been early in the reign, Robert granted to him the forests of Ettrick, Selkirk and Traquair in free barony.

may, however, have been responsible for the one recorded
affray of the whole invasion of 1310–11, when a troop of English
and Welsh infantry was cut off by the Scots while foraging, three
hundred of them being killed before the cavalry could come to
their aid.

In the summer of 1311, with nothing achieved and unable
longer to withstand the clamour for a parliament, Edward returned
south. He had been gone barely a month when Robert followed
him across the border (*Lanercost Chronicle*):

> The said Robert, taking note that the King and all the nobles
> of the realm were in such distant parts [London, where
> Edward was holding a turbulent parliament] and in such
> discord about that accursed individual [Gaveston], having
> collected a large army, invaded England by the Solway on
> Thursday before the feast of the Assumption and burnt all
> the land of the lord of Gilsland, and the town of Haltwhistle,
> and a great part of Tynedale, and after eight days returned
> into Scotland, taking with him a very large booty in cattle.

For fifteen years with only brief intermission Scotland had endured
a war that, save in the first two years, had scarcely touched her
enemy's soil. Now England's turn was beginning. The northern
counties had hardly drawn breath when the Scots reappeared,
this time on the middle marches, swept down Redesdale and
ravaged that part of Tynedale they had previously spared before
returning well satisfied home. These hard successive blows
terrified the Northumbrians into sending to beg a truce. Robert
was agreeable, on terms: two thousand pounds for a truce until
the beginning of February. They bought it, thus giving him
satisfactory proof that he had discovered a means of financing his
operations at his enemy's cost. The English having made the war,
the English should pay for it.

By the beginning of 1312 English and pro-English holdings in
Scotland outside Lothian and Galloway had shrunk to Perth,
Dundee, Stirling and Bothwell. The machinery of government
was in running order, normal diplomatic relations with foreign
countries were in process of re-establishment—with France they
had been resumed as early as 1309—and the prosecution of the
war was one only, albeit an important one, of the king's concerns.
By the summer of that year Robert, holding parliament at Ayr,

might indeed have seemed more king in his kingdom than Edward, now flying from place to place in his, with the favourite on whose destruction the most powerful of the English magnates were irrevocably bent. No English incursion need be expected this year, and Robert could take advantage of his enemies' domestic preoccupations to ravage their soil again. In August the Scots poured over the border, scorching and plundering their way down Tynedale to burn Hexham—again—and Corbridge. At Corbridge Robert halted, his own troops spreading out to devastate Northumberland. Edward Bruce and Douglas swept on under cover of night to fall on Chester-le-Street sleeping, fire the town and race on, still outdistancing word of their approach, to Durham. In the capital of the palatine bishopric it was market day, and the townsfolk were unsuspectingly bustling about the streets when the Scots swooped on them. There was no time or thought for defence. The people took refuge in castle and cathedral on their unassailable rock while the Scots, 'cruelly killing all who opposed them',* methodically pillaged stalls and houses before setting fire to the roofs and marching off, their horses sagging under loads of plunder, to rejoin the king.

Once more the indirect gain of a Scottish raid equalled the direct. The people of Durham, 'fearing more mischief and despairing of help from the King',† paid two thousand pounds for a truce till the following June, as again did the Northumbrians; poorer Westmorland could raise only a part of the sum, and gave hostages for the payment of the rest. Nor were the truce-buyers left in any doubt as to Robert's further intentions, for it was a condition of the truce that the Scots should have free access and retreat through the bishopric of Durham whenever they wished to make a raid into England. The pattern adumbrated the previous year was becoming set. The Scots would, when they could, ravage and rob any English territory not covered by truce. Worthwhile in themselves for their harvest of spoil, for the improvement of morale and the fettling up of Scots troops in excellent field training operations, these raids would serve a wider purpose in wringing from the English in tribute the funds needed to sustain war against them.

Much of the money thus secured was probably invested in siege equipment. The remaining English holdings in Scotland were all,

* *Lanercost Chronicle.* † *CDS*, vol. ii.

inevitably, strongly fortified, and the war at home was now predominantly a matter of reducing them one by one, a necessity that suggested armament for siege. Douglas, apparently, did not hold this view. Throughout his career he seems never to have undertaken a siege save on the king's direct instructions, and alone among the leading Scottish captains never equipped himself with a siege-train. Probably a distaste for the static and largely open operations entailed was fostered by his talent for mobile warfare, but the opinion deducible from his conduct could have been a reasoned one. Siege assaults were in fact very seldom successful. It had taken Edward I, with the strongest and most modern artillery money could buy, and with no risk from any enemy outside, three months to carry Stirling Castle in 1304, and the best of the Scots munitions were inferior to his. Of the fortresses captured by Robert and his lieutenants, not one is known to have fallen to open assault.

Though Douglas acquired no siege engines, he was interested in equipment that could serve his own tactics against fortified places. He had in his following a man called Sim of Ledhouse, apparently one of his professional troopers, who besides being a first-class soldier was a skilled technician. Sim and Douglas put their heads together and between them evolved a device that was to impress contemporaries deeply. This was a collapsible scaling ladder, made of rope-sided steps of wood hanging from an angle of iron pierced with a socket in which a spear-point could be inserted to lift the ladder top and hook the angle on to the wall to be climbed. This contrivance, 'of wondrous construction', less obtrusive and more easily portable than a rigid ladder, was also safer in use, for the placing of weight on the rungs only caused the hook to grip more firmly. It is astonishing, all the same, that anything so simple should have appeared so remarkable an invention. The early fourteenth century was no happy time in Britain, but there is something to be said for an age to which a folding ladder represents a significant advance in military technology.

By the winter of 1312-13 the Douglas-Ledhouse ladder was ready for use. The Scots observed no close season in war. It was in summer that kings were wont to make war, said a contemporary English chronicler (the author of *Vita Edwardi Secundi*), but not the King of Scots. At the beginning of December Robert was laying siege to Perth and Douglas planning to try out his ladders on the biggest prize within his reach, Berwick. Approaching under cover of night on 6 December, he had two ladders in position on the castle wall and the ascent was beginning when a dog barked above and watchmen were heard running to see what had alerted it. Douglas, not the man to risk his troops in a probably doomed attack, promptly called off the operation, leaving the ladders to be discovered, hauled in and triumphantly displayed on a pillory in the town. There they were seen and much admired by the then author of the *Lanercost Chronicle*, who confided to his record a description so full and precise that it could be used as a specification today.*

Berwick was a setback, but a bloodless one at least, and Douglas was not given to repining. The failure there was in any case soon followed by good news from the north. The king, having lulled the alertness of Perth's defenders by ostensibly raising the siege and departing after six fruitless weeks, had returned covertly on the night of 8 January, led his troops through the icy moat at a point where he had previously noted its shallowness, scaled the wall and captured the city. A month later Dumfries fell, bringing Galloway wholly under his control, and in June, after a campaign of less than a month, he regained for Scotland the Isle of Man.

His brother Edward had meanwhile laid siege to Stirling Castle. Formidable on its rock, the fortress that had withstood Edward I for three months was not to be battered down by a little Scottish siege-train, and the best hope of its capture lay in close investment until the garrison was starved into surrender. This was not a process that appealed to the king's impatient brother. He was therefore ready to listen when the constable of Stirling, Sir Philip Mowbray, proposed a truce in which he should be entitled to seek relief from England, the castle to be surrendered unless a relieving force came within three leagues of it by a given date; which, he suggested, should be midsummer day in the following year. Edward agreed, and cheerfully raised the siege. Arrangements of

* He ascribes this attempt to Robert; the author of the *Vita Edwardi Secundi*, written about twelve years later, ascribes it to Douglas. The assailants got away unseen, and the later author may have had information lacking to the English at the time. The ladders are clearly those Barbour describes as evolved by Douglas and Sim, and Barbour's account of the siege of Perth (IX, 359-70) indicates that Robert must have been there at the time of the attempt on Berwick.

this kind were not uncommon in the Middle Ages, their aim being to avert the bloodshed involved in repeated assault and repulse, but they were apt, too, to result in pitched battles between assailants and relievers and this—as Robert perceived at once when the agreement was reported to him—was only too likely a consequence here.

He was furious. His Fabian strategy had more than proved its worth. Save for Lothian and a few fortresses islanded in hostile country, all Scotland had been regained, enemy occupation having been eroded so gradually that no single advance had shocked the quarrelling English into a concerted attempt at reconquest. Now his brother had not merely invited the long-avoided confrontation, but had given the English fantastically long notice to prepare for it. He had, moreover, done this at a time when internal discord in England was in process of resolution. The killing of Gaveston the previous year had, besides eliminating the chief theme of conflict between Edward and his barons, swung to his side the more moderate among them and opened the way to a reconciliation which, however superficial in some respects, might form the basis of a genuine unity in the face of a challenge from Scotland. This challenge had been given without his knowledge, honour forbade its withdrawal, and there was little chance that it would be ignored.

Robert nevertheless continued his customary patient tactics. Abroad, tribute must be gained; this time mere mobilization on the border was enough to frighten the northern counties of England into offering 'no small sum of money, indeed a very large one' (*Lanercost Chronicle*) for a fifteen-month truce. At home his captains turned their attention to Lothian, now the sole district of Scotland in which his writ did not run. Lothian had become a cockpit. Robbed and pillaged by the nationalist Scots, who were said to have inflicted losses worth £20,000 in three years, plundered as occupied territory by the English garrisons of Roxburgh and Berwick, who enriched themselves by capturing the locals, holding them to ransom and killing those who could not pay, the once wealthy province was near ruin. The Lothianers had not even the relief available to the northern English, for when they scraped up their money and bought a truce the people responsible for it were kidnapped by the warden and garrison of Berwick. And when Adam of Gordon went with the aldermen and commune of Roxburgh to see Roxburgh's Gascon constable and complain of his men's conduct he was promptly clapped into prison, 'which has astonished all his [Edward's] good people of Scotland'. So wrote the earl of March and the released Gordon in a statement of Lothian's sufferings which, unable to find redress nearer home, they sent to King Edward in the autumn of that year. For answer they were told it was Edward's intention to lead an army to their relief the following midsummer. The challenge of Stirling had been accepted.

At some time that winter Thomas Randolph laid siege to Edinburgh Castle. Randolph was now earl of Moray, having received the title—in abeyance since the last mormaer* of Moray had died fighting against the Crown in the eleventh century— with a grant of extensive lands in the district, from Robert the previous year. This measure may reflect, besides the king's judgment of his nephew's potential and his normal desire as a fourteenth-century monarch to enrich and employ his own kin, a move to advance his control of the Highlands; Robert's ablest and strongest supporters belonged by birth, as he did himself, to the south-west. The promotion was to prove amply justified.

While Moray invested Edinburgh, Douglas was prowling about Roxburgh. This town, guarded on two sides by the confluent Teviot and Tweed, was covered on the third by one of the strongest castles in Scotland. Roxburgh Castle turned on its approaches a front to deter a general fonder of siege warfare than Douglas, and overlooked pasture land not to be traversed unobserved by assailants whose nearness was, thanks to some skirmishing in the neighbourhood, known to the defenders, and whose aims could well be guessed. That he could scarcely hope to reach the walls unnoticed Douglas knew, but it had occurred to him that to be noticed was not necessarily to be detected.

As twilight fell on Fastern's Eve, Shrove Tuesday, 27 February, he rode down with his men towards Roxburgh. Not far short of the town they dismounted; the archers and the horses were left in concealment and with his men-at-arms, all of them wearing like himself black tunics over their armour, and some with folding

---

* The mormaers (a word variously interpreted as meaning 'sea officers' and 'great stewards') were the provincial governors of the formerly Pictish areas of pre-feudal Scotland. The title was subsequently replaced by 'earl'.

ladders hung against their bodies, Douglas continued on foot. As the castle came in view he dropped to hands and knees, and so did they, spreading out as if at random over the pasture but always moving in their seemingly aimless crawl nearer to its walls. The dark shapes were of course observed by the patrol there, but the mind tends to translate the seen into the familiar, and what the watchmen saw was a herd of black cattle ungathered and forgotten at nightfall. Someone remarked that farmer so-and-so must be drinking deep and, speculating agreeably on the goodman's feelings when he woke to find Douglas had lifted his beasts, they strolled away along the battlements. Their voices receded and died, and the nearest steer stood cautiously upright. The others gathered; ladders were unslung and the first went up on a spear-point till the hook fell snugly over the wall and gripped. Sim of Ledhouse started up.

But the chink of metal on stone had caught the ear of one of the guards who, turning back to investigate, rounded the corner as Sim's head rose above the parapet. Braver than sensible, he did not pause to shout to his fellows but flew at the invader with an impetuosity that carried him half across the wall. Sim seized him by the throat and for a few seconds they grappled; then Sim managed to reach his dagger, the guard's body dropped down among the gathered Scots, and Sim went over the parapet. An instant later another watchman appeared, but Sim was ready for him, and as Douglas and the rest came over the wall the newcomer in his turn was struck down. All was quiet now but for snatches of music drifting up through the darkness.

The castle's occupants, all but the patrol, were making the most of the Shrovetide festival. Bent on enjoyment, they filled the great hall with dancing and singing and playing of games, determined to revel to the full before Lent set in. The party was at its height when across the music there sounded the clanging of metal, and the fierce cry of 'Douglas!' rose up, *inside* the castle. The music broke off, the dancers scattered, and Douglas and his troop burst in. The bemused garrison made little effort at defence. Sir Guillemin de Fenes, the Gascon constable, with a few of his men, managed to reach the keep and barricade himself in, but the rest of the castle was seized almost at once and Douglas, once possessed of the gate, could bring in reinforcements to tackle the keep at leisure.

His men were ganging to and fro
Throughout the castle all that night.

Its defenders held out till the next day when, Fenes having been badly wounded in the face by an arrow, they surrendered on a promise of life and liberty. Douglas himself escorted them to the border, a courtesy perhaps held advisable for their protection; the local population had good cause to hate them, and few tears can have been shed for Fenes in Lothian when he died soon after from the effects of his wound. Sim of Ledhouse was given the enjoyable task of carrying the news of Roxburgh's fall to Robert, who 'made him full great rewarding', and sent Edward Bruce with his siege-train to 'tumble down' the castle.

The capture of Roxburgh decisively altered the balance of power in Teviotdale, causing such alarm that the English abbot and canons of Jedburgh fled to England the very day they heard the news. Jedburgh Castle was still in English hands, and seems to have resisted an attack by Douglas soon after, but the churchmen were probably wise to flee; there was little security in Scotland now for unarmed Englishmen outside fortifications.

Moray heard of Roxburgh's fall at Edinburgh, where he was still laying siege to the castle. This was known as the Maidens' Castle from its deemed impregnability, and Moray was beginning to understand why. The news of Roxburgh's fall, and its method, struck spurs into his will. The two young captains had become close friends, but affection did not preclude emulousness, and if Douglas had succeeded at Roxburgh Moray must not fail at Edinburgh. A promise of reward for anyone telling him a secret way into the Maidens' Castle evoked a man called William Francis, son of a former captain of the castle, who as a lustful lad had nightly climbed in and out to visit a mistress in the town, and who thought he could remember his route. On a black night a diversionary assault was mounted on the east gate, while under the north face of the Rock Moray, Francis and thirty picked men gathered to tackle, mailed and in darkness, an ascent perilous by day. They succeeded; after a hideous moment when, as they paused to puff on a ledge half-way up, a passing English watchman called gaily and untruthfully, 'I see you', they reached and crossed the parapet, made their way down, took the East Port's defenders in the rear and let in their comrades to seize the Maidens' Castle.

Edinburgh fell in March. That same month Edward II issued his writs of summons to the army that was 'to put down and suppress the wicked rebellion of Robert Bruce and his accomplices in the King's land of Scotland'.*

* *Rotuli Scotiae*, translation by G. W. S. Barrow, *Robert Bruce and the Community of the Realm of Scotland.*

Chapter 5

Bannockburn

> The victory of battle standeth not in the multitude of a host, but strength cometh from heaven.
> They come against us in much pride and iniquity to destroy us, and our wives and children, and to spoil us.
> But we fight for our lives and our laws.
>
> I Maccabees

This time Edward meant business. The magnates of England had been summoned to bring their quotas of knight service for the reduction of Scotland; writs had been issued for troops to be levied in the northern and midland counties of England (the southern ones would have to supply men in the event of a French war); Wales and Ireland had been called on; twenty-one sheriffdoms had been ordered to supply the waggons needed to transport the army's baggage, ships had been requisitioned to carry the more perishable supplies to Scotland by sea, and word had gone abroad that knights seeking adventure and spoil were welcome in Edward's enterprise. Wark on the Tweed was named for the muster, and 10 June the appointed date. On 17 June Edward was at Berwick with all his appurtenances of war: knights, archers, infantry; auxiliaries, among them grooms, blacksmiths and carpenters; servants and camp-followers; a train of waggons that, placed end to end, would, it was reckoned, have stretched for twenty leagues; pavilions for the royal bivouac; tableware of gold, and a Carmelite versifier to hymn his great victory when he had won it.

Not all the baronage of England was present. The most hostile of the earls had refused attendance on the ground of Edward's failure to seek parliamentary sanction for his undertaking, but they had sent their contingents, while Aymer de Valence, now earl of Pembroke, the young earl of Gloucester—Edward's nephew and the Bruces' cousin—and Edward's brother-in-law the earl of Hereford were present in person. The absence of the hostile magnates did little to diminish the splendour of the host gathered at Berwick. 'There were in that assemblage', wrote an English chronicler,* 'enough men to traverse all Scotland, and in the judgment of some, if the whole of Scotland had been brought together it could not make a stand against the army of the King. Indeed, it was confessed by the whole host, that in our time such an army had not gone out of England.'

King Robert's hosting had begun in May in the Torwood, a tract of woodland stretching from Falkirk north to the Bannock burn about two-and-a-half miles south of Stirling and westward into the Kilsyth hills, and thither Douglas had marched with his veterans. It was largely with professional soldiers of this ilk that Robert intended to meet the English attack; if indeed he met it, for, still undecided between fighting and withdrawal, he was keeping both alternatives in mind. Seven years earlier he had accepted that the Scots could never meet the English on their own cavalry-centred terms, and should he resolve on battle his strategy would be founded on the infantry in schiltrom (see p. 55). These troops would not, however, be confined to regular spearmen. Unlike their peers in richer countries, Scottish knights had long been used to fighting on foot and saw in it no derogation from their dignity. In Bruce's army noblemen and gentry would stand shoulder to shoulder with troopers and with any burgesses or yeomen able to furnish the necessary equipment and fit to wield it, in a democracy of battle still unknown to the rest of Europe.

Schiltrom formations were essentially defensive and, employed by Wallace at Falkirk, had been countered by Edward I's use of his Welsh bowmen to splinter the schiltroms at long range until the English cavalry could move in to complete their destruction. Mindful of Falkirk, Robert had evolved various tactics for use against a possible repetition. One of these was to render the schiltrom mobile, and in the waiting weeks in the Torwood his troops

* *Vita Edwardi Secundi*, translated by N. Denholm-Young.

were drilled to manoeuvre in formation while maintaining unbroken their defensive thicket of spearpoints.

The archers would be mobilized separately, as would the small troop of hobelars or light horse—mailed troops riding mounts too light to carry armour of their own, as did the true war-horses—under the Marischal's command. The infantry, his chief arm, Robert organized in four divisions, one under his own command, one under his brother Edward, one under Moray, while the fourth was Douglas's. Douglas, however, was asked technically to share his command. His young cousin Walter, Steward of Scotland since old James's death five years earlier,* was now of fighting age and had brought his own retinue and vassals to the muster. Convention precluded the Steward's subordination to a commander of inferior social rank, and the king therefore asked Douglas to accept nominal joint command of a division for whose handling he would of course be responsible in practice. He seems to have accepted this cheerfully enough; the Scots put first things first. Less happy was the response of the earl of Hereford, constable of England, to a not dissimilar situation caused by King Edward's decision to grant the young earl of Gloucester joint command with Hereford of his vanguard, and the resultant dissension between the two earls became a talking-point in the great army now sweating its slow way over the Lammermoors.

On Saturday 22 June the English were reported advancing from Edinburgh, and Robert moved his army northward towards Stirling along the road Edward could be expected to take the next day. Emerging from the Torwood they could see before them the road to Stirling as the English would see it in their turn. From the woodland the road dipped to ford the Bannock burn where it ran out of the westward hills to plunge, east of the ford, between steep banks on its way past the settlement called Bannockburn and thence to wind into marshy flats, tide-washed in the lower reaches, till it joined the no less winding Forth. Beyond the ford the road ascended to enter trees again, the woodland in the New Park, Stirling Castle's hunting-ground, that King Alexander had enclosed fifty years earlier. Passing through the eastern fringe of this woodland, the road ran by St Ninian's Kirk just beyond the trees and straight on to Stirling. East of the road lay a belt of cultivated ground extending as far as Stirling, which at its farther

* Walter's elder brother Andrew had predeceased his father.

edge sloped steeply to the Carse, a great expanse of swampy flatland that filled the triangle whose other sides were the Bannock and the Forth. The Carse even at midsummer was soggy with the waters of many small streams running down from the westward hills to ooze their way through the flats to Bannock or Forth; no large body of horse could cross it, nor could they safely traverse the hilly and broken country westward of the New Park. The English must approach Stirling either by the road or by the firm land that lay between road and Carse, and it was Robert's expectation that Edward, confident in his power, would choose the road.

Here among the trees of the New Park the Scots could meet him on ground where neither cavalry nor longbowmen could be used to the best advantage. Nor should they have to contend with natural obstacles alone. To reinforce the aid he expected from his chosen site, the king, on reaching the New Park, set his men to digging holes in the open land where the road rose from the ford to the Park, till the ground was honeycombed with a cavalry trap designed to bring down the first English comers and funnel later assaults on to the narrow front that would give his infantry most chance of rebuffing them. All night the digging went on, and in the morning the pits, carefully masked with sticks and grass, were inspected and approved by Robert himself.

The Scots slept in the New Park that night, and the next morning rose early. It was Sunday and a fast day, the eve of St John, and battle or no battle it would be kept on bread and water. The army heard mass and the pious, or the prudent, were shriven. Then Robert spoke to his troops. The prospect ahead, he told them, was hard fighting, to be endured only by the wholehearted; if any hesitated to face it, let him depart. The call of Henry V before Agincourt, it met a like response, a general shout of readiness to take whatever should come. So reassured, he set about his dispositions. The 'small folk'—servants, camp-followers and the fighting men who were not equipped or trained to fight in schiltrom—he sent with the baggage to the valley between Gillies and Coxet Hills, half a mile west of the road, to await the outcome. At the entry to the Park he stationed his own division, to take the brunt of the expected assault. He had not, however, overlooked the possibility of an out-flanking movement along the open land east of the Park, and Moray's schiltrom he posted by St Ninian's Kirk to deal with any such attempt. Edward Bruce's division and Douglas's were between these two—Edward nearer the king in the entry, Douglas nearer Moray—ready to aid whichever seemed more in need. All being in readiness, Robert asked Douglas and the Marischal to reconnoitre the advancing enemy.

With their equerries they rode back through the Torwood as far as Falkirk, and took up a position where they could see and study the English army.

> And soon the great host have they seen
> Where shields shining were so sheen,
> And bascinets well burnished bright
> That gave against the sun great light.
> They saw so many broad banners,
> Standards, pennons there and spears,
> So many knights upon steeds,
> All flaming there in their weeds,
> So many battles [divisions] and so broad,
> That took so much room as they rode,
> That the maist host and the stoutest
> Of Christendom, and eke the best,
> Should be dismayed there to see
> Their foes in-to such quantity.

Most conspicuous as most important were the knights, the mailed warriors on mailed destriers—great stallions more like Clydesdales than any saddle-horse of today—that were the tanks of the time, man and horse operating as one entity trained to ride down any opposition and overcome by weight as much as by weaponry. Edward's knights hailed not from England only but from Wales, Ireland, Gascony, a few from France or Hainault, one or two even from Germany, so widespread were hopes of sharing the fun and the spoil of his great conquest, and these were only a part of his army. There were light horsemen to match the little troop that was Scotland's whole cavalry, crossbowmen, longbowmen, pike-carrying infantry, unreeling for mile on mile in the greatest army England had sent forth in living memory.

> They were too many sure to fight
> The few folk of a simple land.

Keith and Douglas gazed at them with sinking hearts. Conscious though they were that the Scots must be outnumbered, they had not imagined such odds as these. Staring down the seemingly endless line, they reckoned that it must hold three English to one Scot, while the disproportion in armaments was far greater.* They cantered back to the New Park, sought out the king and told him in private what impression the English had made on them. He heard them out and warned them not to speak of it to anyone else; the morale of his outnumbered, out-munitioned army must not be imperilled. If questioned they were to say that the English seemed tired, and were advancing in poor order.

The long, hot day wore on. With the other captains Douglas stood near the king at the New Park's entry, gazing across the Bannock for the appearance of the enemy van. But when the first English were sighted it was not on the road down to the ford, and it was Robert himself who observed a movement down on the edge of the Carse to their left. It shaped itself into a brigade of English cavalry under the banners of lord Clifford and Sir Henry Beaumont which, having evidently diverged from the main road back in the Torwood and crossed the burn well east of the ford, was now riding up to take the level ground and advance towards Stirling by St Ninian's Kirk. This was the movement Moray had been posted to handle, and there was Moray, not even with his division but among the group of captains staring across to the Torwood. Grimly Robert pointed out to his nephew what he had seen, with the words, 'A rose has fallen from your chaplet'. The horrified earl raced for his schiltrom and with his staff and his captains Robert followed, and at the eastern edge of the wood halted to watch as Moray formed up his men and marched them out.

The English were already past the point at which he should have intercepted them, and could easily have left the slower footsoldiers impotent behind them. But their commanders evidently shared Edward Bruce's code of chivalry. At sight of the schiltrom bustling after them, plainly anxious for battle, the Englishmen paused and turned to face the Scots. An instant later, as Moray

* Barbour, who states that there were 100,000 English to 30,000 Scots, is, like all chroniclers of his time, not to be trusted with figures over a thousand; his estimates are impossibly high. His ratio, however, may be near the mark. Professor Barrow (*Robert Bruce and the Community of the Realm of Scotland*) reckons that the English may have numbered some 15–16,000 foot and 2,500 horse of all kinds to the Scots' 5–6,000 foot and 500 light horse.

halted his men and faced them outwards to present a bristle of spears in every direction, lances were levelled and the destriers lumbered into a charge. In a few moments the schiltrom was encircled, and the onlookers in the wood could see little but the huge shapes of the horsemen manoeuvring about and plunging into a cloud of dust, where only the din of continuing battle and an occasional waving spearpoint could tell them Moray's division still stood.

To the anxiously watching Douglas it seemed they could not do so long without reinforcement. As the English charged again and again at the dust-shrouded patch of ground held by the schiltrom, alarm took increasing possession of him till at last, unable longer to bear the sight, he went to the king and asked permission to take his own troop to Moray's aid; and got an unhesitating no. Robert had good reason for this. A large part of his total strength was here engaged with a lesser proportion of the English, and to throw in Douglas's division would commit nearly half his resources when the main English army might at any moment debouch from the Torwood ready for battle. Further, Moray's engagement had vouchsafed a field trial of the tactics on which he had chosen to depend. If, fighting at better odds than the Scots army could expect as a whole, Moray failed to hold his ground, there could be no question of giving Edward battle.

All this should have been plain to Douglas himself. His normal serenity, however, had failed under pressure on what seems to have been his one real and ultimately fatal weakness in battle: inability to preserve his judgment in face of a friend's danger. Now apparently blind to everything but his conviction that Moray was being destroyed while he stood by inactive, he persisted in his demand till the king unwillingly yielded with a proviso that he must disengage as soon as he might reasonably do so. Robert departed then, to see how matters stood at the other end of his position, while Douglas in his turn formed up his division and marched it out into the open. Before even reaching the battle-ground he knew that he had wholly misjudged the situation.

The English were certainly full of sound and fury, but it was the sound and fury of a pack of hounds round a porcupine. They could not get at the vulnerable parts of their prey. The pikemen's one advantage of reach was proving total, the horses that charged them being impaled before their riders could touch the Scots.

Each unavailing assault had brought down more destriers and left the surviving beasts harder to manage, till by the time Douglas was forming up his men the English had in desperation been reduced to throwing their hand weapons, quite ineffectively, at the Scots. Milling in bafflement about their firmly planted adversaries, they became aware that another porcupine was marching to join the first, wavered in dismay and gave back a little. Douglas saw the movement, and understood his mistake. At once he halted his troop, declaring that they must not join in a battle already all but won; Moray and his men had earned and must enjoy the full glory of their victory. Moray, meanwhile, observing the English recoil, had marshalled his schiltrom for attack. They now advanced firmly against the disordered knights who, wholly demoralized, scattered and fled, some for the castle and some back towards the main English army. Pursuit was impossible, and the victorious and panting Scots paused to pull off their helmets and mop their sweat-drenched faces before turning back to the wood and the joyous congratulations of Douglas and his men.

At the other end of the Scottish line the tensest moment of the war had come and gone. As the English van emerged from the Torwood, Robert, astride the grey pony on which he had been hacking about his position, and armed only with a battleaxe, had ridden out to study the advancing enemy, been challenged by Sir Henry Bohun and, hazarding Scotland's whole hope on a single stroke, had met the challenge. The outrageous gamble had paid off. Bohun, his lance missing its target as the handy little pony swung aside, fell dead from the saddle under a single savage blow of Robert's axe and the king's division, letting out the breath that every man must have been holding in dread, thereupon marched out of the wood to engage and drive back across the Bannock the dismayed English. Robert withdrew his men to their position again, and awaited the next move. No further advance was made along the road, and after a while the English could be seen emerging from the Torwood to the east and beginning to cross the Bannock farther down, towards the Carse and not far from the settlement called Bannockburn. The river crossed, the forward movement ceased. They spread about the marshland, horsemen dismounted, packhorses began to be unloaded, tents to rise. The English were pitching camp.

It was now clear to Robert that there would be no battle on

his chosen site. The move into the Carse had probably been dictated by the need for water, but it could not now be expected that on the morrow Edward would return to the road approach. Clifford's humiliating repulse by St Ninian's had at least bought the knowledge of another way to Stirling fit for the passage of cavalry, and it now seemed reasonably certain that Edward would advance to the castle along the open ground between the New Park and the Carse, where the Scots, if they still chose to fight, would lack the protection of woodland and the pit-narrowed front prepared at the entry to the Park. Robert's preparations nevertheless had served a turn. He still had a choice. Should he now follow the course of prudence, leave Stirling's recapture to another day and withdraw to the wild country westward where pursuit would be impossible, he could take with him an undefeated army cheerful in the knowledge that the English had been twice discomfited, and leave a humiliated enemy behind him. Yet should he venture still to press his luck, advantage could be reaped from Edward's choice of bivouac. Moving so large an army to the firm ground above the Carse and dressing it there for battle would be a lengthy process; if the Scots could attack in time they might succeed in hemming the enemy in to a site too narrow for adequate deployment, with the treacherous ground of the Carse at their backs.

It was not Robert Bruce's way to impose his unquestionable will on those who must execute it. Having weighed up the possibilities, he called his troops about him and laid the choice before them. The answer came unanimously: fight.

At about three o'clock the next morning, 24 June, the last day for Stirling's relief, Douglas and the Steward stood harnessed for battle before their schiltrom on the eastern fringe of the New Park woodland. The incomplete darkness of midsummer night was already fading from the sky, and down on the edge of the Carse, perhaps half a mile distant and a little to their right, the English could be seen beginning to break camp. Their division now formed the Scottish left; the army had been faced about to the new front and its dispositions redrawn, so that Edward Bruce's schiltrom was now on the right and nearest to the English, Moray's in the centre and Douglas's next to it, with Robert's own division held in reserve. They had heard mass and sparsely breakfasted, and had taken up their formations with standards raised. The king had commanded that all be ready by sunrise, and ready they were.

As if to emphasize the solemnity of the occasion, Robert opened the day by conferring a number of knighthoods before the assembled army, both Douglas and the Steward being among those honoured. In the case of Douglas the ceremony was probably that of elevation to the rank of banneret,* conferable only on the battlefield, which was symbolically granted by the king's slashing off with his sword the forks of the knight's pennon to convert it into the square standard of the banneret. The ceremonial done, Robert moved out before his army to address to them his final exhortation. The die was cast, and they were about to meet in open battle the over-weening might of the English. They were few against many, yet the advantage lay with them. Their cause was just, and God would uphold the right. They were fighting on their own soil, defending their homes, their wives and their children against an enemy who would show no mercy in victory, and that knowledge would strengthen their arms. Let them stand steady with unfailing courage, as well he knew they would, and the English could not overcome. Their prospects were splendid; their enemy had brought into Scotland great wealth for their taking (Robert knew, of course, how the baser as well as the nobler instincts may serve a commander's turn) but they must not let plunder deflect them until the battle was won. Afterward there would be spoil in plenty for all. He concluded by promising that no reliefs (death duties, in effect) would be levied from the heirs of those who fell in the battle, and that pardon would be granted all offenders against the Crown who fought honourably there.

The three schiltroms moved from the wood into the pale light of the rising sun. They marched a short distance, and halted; the abbot of Inchaffray came forward holding aloft St Columba's reliquary, the brecbennoch, and the troops fell to their knees while he prayed. They rose again, and the small, neat formations marched briskly off across the open ground that divided them from the sprawling mass of the English army.

There their emergence on foot had caused surprise approaching incredulity. The English knew, of course, that in default of horse, infantry might be opposed to cavalry, as by Wallace at Falkirk and the Flemings at Courtrai, but they knew too, or thought they

* In the Argyll campaign of 1308 Robert had placed under Douglas's command several knights not his feudal subordinates, which suggests that he had by then been a knight bachelor.

knew, that this expedient of penury allowed defensive tactics only; even at Courtrai the Flemings had not attacked until the French knights had bogged themselves down in a ditch. Despite the warning given by Moray's advance against Clifford the day before, it still seemed outside military possibility for an army of foot-soldiers to open battle by attacking mounted troops. 'What, will these men fight?' exclaimed Edward, staring at the schiltroms; then as they knelt he thought he had the answer. 'See, they kneel to ask mercy.' 'Yes,' answered Ingram Umfraville, the one-time Guardian of Scotland, 'but not of you.' The Scots rose and came on.

They could see the English clearly now, most of the army in one conglomerate mass—a 'great schiltrom', Barbour calls it—heaving and glittering with movement as the trumpets sounded and mailed figures scrambled to horse. A little ahead, the vanguard was hastily forming up, the earl of Gloucester flinging himself surcoatless into the saddle, to charge on Edward Bruce's division as it marched steadily across the open ground. The schiltrom halted, spears at the ready, and the first wave of English knights crashed upon them. Moray's troop was now close, and another breaker surged from the 'great schiltrom' to engulf it,

> So that it seemed well that they
> Were lost among so great meinie,
> As they were plunged in the sea.

As many again were thrusting their way clear of the main host to tackle Douglas's battalion, now marching up on Moray's left. The foremost knights must now have been hardly a stone's-throw from them, metalled pyramids seven foot or more from helmet-crest to hoof, that swung ponderously head-on to the schiltrom to thunder into the charge. Douglas brought his men as near as he could to Moray's, and halted them. Spear-butts were grounded, points advanced and muscles braced against the coming impact, as past the slender pales the foot-soldiers stared at the moving fortresses that pounded down upon them. They grew enormous, filled the sight, towered at spear's length, and were held there.

Charging, the destriers presented armoured fronts to their adversaries, but a prod could stimulate the rearing that exposed unprotected bellies to spearpoint or sword. Flung from a rearing horse, brought down with a piked one, the knight in his heavy armour had little chance, even if he were not stunned, of rising unaided before a Scot pounced from the ranks to dispose of him with sword or axe-blow. To raise and remount a fallen knight was the squire's function, but such aid was hardly possible on this narrow field thronged with other knights trying to batter a way forward to the front and cumbered already with riderless horses running loose and piked ones dead or kicking in agony; Gloucester had already gone down, unidentifiable without his surcoat, to be pounded to death under the feet of his cousin's schiltrom. The Scots fought in grim silence, sparing their breath as they braced spears against the ton weights of armoured muscle that hurtled upon them, but all was pandemonium as the snap of breaking spears, the screams of disembowelled horses and the groans of the wounded rose above the incessant clatter of metal on metal.

Another sound joined the din, a twanging and hissing, and in the schiltroms men reeled with arrow-shafts springing from their bodies. Someone had managed to marshal the longbowmen and position them on the English flank with a clear line of fire towards the Scots. Unshielded now by forest, the spearmen could only fight on and pray that Robert's counter would work. It was already on its way; from behind them came the hoofbeats of horses ridden fast and orderly. The Marischal with his five hundred light horse swept past the interlocked armies, levelled lance and drove into the longbowmen. Some fell, others fled—many to be struck down by English knights still struggling to get to the front—and all were scattered. Their part magnificently played, Keith and his horsemen trotted back to the rear and the Scottish archers, no longer menaced by adversaries who outranged them, moved into position to add their quota to the growing confusion in the English ranks.

Pressing closer together as they fought, the three schiltroms were now almost in line. The English assaults, unorganized from the start and impeded now by their own dead strewing a ground so narrow that little momentum could be built up, were weakening and growing more sporadic. The Scots began to move forward, their footing cautious on the battle floor that had become a shambles.

> Many that strong were, and hardy,
> Down under foot lying all dead
> Where all the field of blood was red.

The bastion of spears inched forward nevertheless, and the throng of knights churning confusedly before it gave back a little. At this the resolute silence of the Scots broke in excitement with cries of 'On them! They fail!' The line pushed forward again. From behind, a well-known war-cry rose to join their shouts, and a fourth schiltrom thrust up on the flank. Robert, seeing the scales begin to tip, had brought in the reserve. Joined in one line, their moving palisade unbroken by the increasingly frantic thrusts against it, the Scots pressed steadily on. Among the English confusion was growing anarchic as some still strove towards the front, others away from the inexorably closing ring of spearpoints, and all were forced back on the treacherous ground of the Carse. Beyond the battleground what remained of the 'great schiltrom' was beginning to disintegrate as men fled back to the main camp and through it, over the Carse towards Stirling or southward in search of the Bannockburn crossing where many, coming unawares in their panicked flight to the river in ravine, would plunge over the bank to die in a heap of struggling men and horses that was to choke 'Bannockburn betwixt the braes' till a man could cross dryshod. Then came the visible signal of defeat. The standard of England, the leopard banner of the Plantagenets, was moving away from the battlefield towards Stirling.

Douglas saw the movement, and knew it must be followed. His men had no more need of him; his schiltrom was part of a machine mowing its steady way into what of the English army was left in the fight. He withdrew and hurried to the rear, where Robert was watching and assessing the movements of the defeated troops while past him poured what might at a distance have seemed another army. The light troops and servants left to wait in the New Park had watched the battle with excitement rising till they could bear inaction no longer and, choosing leaders among themselves and rigging up blankets on poles to look like banners, came streaming down to join in the rout of the English. The leopard standard was well clear of the battle now, receding fast over the plain towards Stirling with some five hundred mounted men about it, and Douglas asked leave to take the Scottish horse and go in pursuit of the King of England. Robert agreed he should 'take the chase', but would allow him a part only of the cavalry. The surviving English, many of whom had not even taken part in the battle, still greatly outnumbered the Scots, and many of them, having fled over the Carse, were gathering about the Abbey Crag. Robert, by no means certain that he might not have to fight another battle before the day was out, dared not part with more than sixty men.

Edward had meanwhile reached Stirling Castle and sought entrance. The constable, Mowbray, either refused it or advised against it—accounts conflict—because, the castle being now forfeit to the Scots, Edward must if within it become their prisoner. The fugitive king turned away, circled the New Park to the west and plunged into the Torwood. There soon after Douglas followed, still hopeful of capturing with sixty light horse a man guarded by five hundred horsemen, many of whom were fully accoutred knights, but almost certainly aware that only exceptional luck could bring him success.

Before he had gone very far, however, there happened something that must have suggested luck was with him that day. Riding through the Torwood he saw coming towards his troop another of some four score mounted men under the standard of Abernethy, whose late lord, long an adherent of the English, had bequeathed his allegiance to his son. The two parties halted, the leaders rode forward to parley and young Abernethy, asked what he was doing there, said he was bringing his men to join the King of England's army. Douglas joyously told him what had happened to the King of England's army, explained his present enterprise and suggested that Abernethy should now change sides and join him. This Abernethy promptly did, an astonishing volte-face in which he may have been less cynical than overwhelmed; he was very young and Douglas, not at any time an easy man to say no to, must now, hot from the greatest victory Scotland had ever won, have been all but irresistible. Delaying only for the essential ceremony of Abernethy's oath of fealty, they joined their forces and rode on. Douglas had more than doubled his resources, but they still totalled less than a third of Edward's.

The English troop came in sight before they had reached Linlithgow, and Douglas closed upon them until his men were hardly a bowshot behind. They trailed Edward thus as far as Winchburgh where, the English halting to bait their horses, Douglas halted too and baited his in full view of his quarry. He may have had some plan for Edward's capture that entailed exasperating the English into an attack on his little force, for after Winchburgh he became even more provocative, hanging on the heels of the enemy and snapping up any straggler until

> He let them not have such leisure
> As ance water for to make.

But the English were not to be provoked. They had suffered an unexpected and total defeat, and all that now was left them was to avoid the ultimate shame of their king's capture. Riding close about Edward—who was vowing that if he got safely home he would found a Carmelite college—they kept on in their necessary, humiliating flight, leaving to death or capture by Douglas the weary and those whose mounts were spent or lame. They were expendable, and the King of England was not.

Through the long midsummer day that ludicrous chase kept on, the little troop snapping at the heels of the big one like a terrier after a mastiff. Arthur's Seat rose up on the left and fell behind, beyond it the sparkling Forth widened to the sea. To the right appeared the dusty track that was the main road south, climbing up Soutra into the hill country that to Douglas probably offered most chance of entrapping Edward. The English ignored it and kept on eastward. Douglas must have known then that the chance was gone, and known too that his undertaking was hopeless. Edward was not heading for Berwick direct but for Dunbar, sea-castle of that constant English adherent the earl of March, and the only hope that Robert now might gain the trump card of Edward's person lay in March's having sense or cynicism enough to see where his interest lay and act accordingly. March, however, higher-minded or less quick-witted than Abernethy and without Douglas to persuade, remained regrettably true to his fealty. Edward with a few companions vanished into Dunbar Castle, whence shortly they were shipped to Berwick, and the rest of the English started south overland, Douglas solacing himself for his disappointment by securing yet more prisoners from among them. His loss at least was Oxford's gain, for Edward kept the vow made in his flight and Oriel College still bears witness to it.

Chapter 6

Fortis Malleator Anglorum*

> Hush ye, hush ye,
> Little pet ye,
> Hush ye, hush ye,
> Do not fret ye.
> The Black Douglas
> Shall not get ye.
>
> Northumbrian lullaby

Some two hundred knights of England died at Bannockburn, and of Scottish knights two. In its scale, its completeness and its moral effect it was a truly significant victory. In a battle engaging a high proportion of the resources of both combatants an invader had been routed with a totality that was almost at once to render the victory, as it still remains, one of the most cherished national memories of the Scottish people. And there it stopped, for the political consequences of the great victory were negligible. Where Bruce erred was in failing to throw every available man into the drive to capture Edward. With the King of England in his hands he could pretty well have dictated the terms of peace, but Edward at liberty, however defeated, was at liberty to maintain the war. The misjudgment was understandable. To Robert, watching the great English army crumble before his schiltroms, only two possibilities can have presented themselves. Either his victory was less complete than it appeared and there remained a risk of further battle that must be catered for, or he had indeed wholly triumphed and Scottish independence could not but be conceded. One way he dared not, the other he need not commit all his

* Fordun's eulogy of Douglas.

cavalry to Douglas's pursuit. It was probably only as the weeks went by and no envoy came empowered to treat of Scottish independence that he realized the true state of things, that he had won a total victory without ending the war.

In thus maintaining his claim to the crown of a country he dared enter only with an army around him, Edward was acting in a fashion well understood in his time. Claims to property tended to be looked on as themselves a kind of property, to be established if possible and if not to be preserved in the hope that some change in circumstance might permit their success at a later date. A man who voluntarily yielded such a pretension might sincerely feel himself to be impoverishing his heirs. Some day Edward or some later king of England would reconquer his rebellious dominion—till then his claim must be preserved, and if the price of preservation was the ruin of his northern counties he was willing to pay; the north was poor country anyway. His capital and his wealth lay in the south.

That the north should suffer was inevitable. The continuance of the war meant the continuance of Robert's need for money to prosecute it and, naturally, of his determination that England should furnish this. After Bannockburn the northern counties entered on a period of misery unequalled since the Conqueror wasted them as, annually if not oftener, the Scots descended to take tribute from those who would buy immunity and pillage those who would not or could not. The atrocities of Edward I's conquest of Scotland were not imitated, even the English admitting that the Scots killed few who did not resist them. Enrichment, not bloodshed, was the object and they set about it systematically, heading south with spare horses unladen, returning with the money and grain that bought short truces for the English, and the booty of the ravaged districts. These each year had to be sought farther afield across a widening belt of desolation. If they killed few the dearth they left behind them must have killed many, and driven more away. Soon Northumberland was almost uninhabited outside castles and walled towns, so that 'some fifteen years that land lay waste, abandoned by men and given over to wild beasts' (*Melsa Chronicle*). These were the years in which the name of the Black Douglas entered northern folklore.

Almost as soon as the Scots realized that Bannockburn had not won them peace, Douglas was over the border with Edward

Bruce. In August they entered Northumberland and headed south, leaving a wake of blackened fields and burning villages, exacted tribute from the bishopric of Durham and kept on unopposed as far as Richmond before turning north again by Swaledale, with a great booty of cattle and numerous prisoners, to re-enter Scotland by the western marches (*Lanercost Chronicle*).

> Also they burnt the towns of Brough and Appleby and Kirkoswald, and other towns here and there on their route, trampling down the crops by themselves and their beasts as much as they could. But the people of Coupland, fearing their return and invasion, sent envoys and appeased them with much money.

It was probably Douglas too who at the winter solstice led the Scots to attack Gilsland and terrify Tynedale into doing homage to Robert before vanishing once more and leaving the English to a winter of hunger; for in the summer after Bannockburn foul weather had destroyed the crops all over Europe, and famine as well as war was assailing them.

The spring found him more peacefully occupied. In April he accompanied the king on a visit to earl Malcolm of Lennox, and thence to Ayr, where Robert convoked his second parliament since Bannockburn. At the previous gathering, held at Cambuskenneth in November, Robert had issued an ultimatum to all Scottish landowners not yet in his peace, who were required to enter it within a year under pain of forfeiture, thus bringing to his allegiance most of the remaining dissidents whose lands lay predominantly in Scotland, while the forfeitures from those who still refused their fealty—Comyn kindred still unwilling to compound with John Comyn's killer, or nobles whose principal estates lay outside Scotland—would yield him the wherewithal to reward those, Douglas among them, whose services had earned recognition. The chief purpose of the Ayr Parliament was to establish the succession.

Among the indirect consequences of Bannockburn had been the return to Scotland of Robert's one legitimate child, Marjorie, as a result of the surrender of Bothwell. To this castle had fled many of the English who escaped the battle, among them the earl of Hereford, careless that their harbourage there would ensure for the isolated stronghold immediate siege, without hope of relief, by the victorious Scots. Bothwell's constable, Sir Walter Gilbertson, was not so unconcerned for the future. Presumably seeing no reason to endure the rigours of a foredoomed siege, Sir Walter decided not merely to accept the inevitable but to cushion himself against it. Opening the castle gates, he welcomed in Hereford and the more important of his fellow-fugitives, closed the gates behind them and changed sides, thus delivering to Robert a prisoner more valuable than any the battle had brought him. For Hereford was Edward's brother-in-law, and his countess cried at her brother till he promised that to achieve her lord's release she might dispose of all the Scottish prisoners still in his hands. Thus for this one foolish earl there were released to Scotland bishop Wishart, the king's sisters Christian and Mary, and his wife and daughter to become in due course the mothers, one of the last Bruce, the other of the first Stewart king. But although Marjorie was now free and betrothed to the young Steward, the Succession Act of 1315 subordinated her claim to that of Edward Bruce as 'an active man and one experienced in war', on whom the crown was to devolve in default of a male heir of the king's body; should a minor succeed, Moray was to assume the regency.

Edward Bruce at last had in prospect the crown he thought himself well fitted to assume, but it was still being worn by a healthy brother less than a year his senior. Edward wanted a kingdom now, and as it happened he had one in his eye. The subking of Tyrone had sent to ask Scottish aid in driving the English out of Ireland, with a promise of the high kingship of Ireland for Edward Bruce if he could achieve it. This Edward was confident he could do. Robert endorsed an ambition which, besides offering the chance, one he felt Scotland now capable of using, of a second front against England, had the ancillary charm of removing his brother from the realm; Scotland was becoming too small for the two of them. In May Edward sailed for Ireland, accompanied by Moray and a crowd of warriors eager for adventure and spoil in this new field.

Douglas was not among them. Whether or not he would have liked to join a campaign into fresh country, the office he now held as Warden of the Marches* kept him at home. In times of peace

---

* It is not known when he received this office; both Barbour and the *Scotichronicon* mention him as controlling the marches in the years after Bannockburn. The latter describes him as 'Custos Marchiarum', which suggests that he held a single wardenship over the three marches—east, middle and west—later separately wardened.

the warden's function was to maintain order on the marches, secure the observance of the border laws and, in concert with his opposite number in England, adjudicate disputes between marchmen from either side, but now it was, inevitably, defence. This to Douglas naturally comprehended attack. In June he was off south again, this time to Hartlepool. His direction may have been imposed by Robert, who had a grudge against this town for capturing a ship taking armour and food to the Scots; he had refused to sell the burgesses a truce, and now the townsfolk could only take refuge in ships out at sea while Douglas sacked their homes. Returned with plunder, and prisoners taken for purposes of ransom, he and his men were towards the end of July summoned to join the king in laying siege to Carlisle.

Why Robert sought to capture an English town when Berwick was still unredeemed is not known; the English believed him to be moved by a desire to avenge his brothers, Thomas and Alexander, who had suffered execution there. It was a considerable undertaking for the Scots with their paucity of siege equipment to invest any fortified town, let alone one in England where the likelihood of relief was strong and the chance of reducing the town by attrition thus negligible. Realizing perhaps that Carlisle must be taken swiftly if at all, Robert set about the assault with great energy. Daily the Scots attacked one of the city gates, and sometimes all three at once, but always to be beaten back 'with such dense volleys of darts and arrows, likewise stones, that they asked one another whether stones bred and multiplied within the walls' (*Lanercost Chronicle*). Though Bruce and Douglas may not then have realized it, they were confronting in the governor of Carlisle the only Englishman of their time who was of their own calibre as a soldier. He was Andrew Harcla, a Westmorland knight who had already shown himself readier than most of the demoralized northern gentry to attempt retaliation for the Scottish raids, and whom this siege had given the first real chance to show the stuff he was made of. Speeding his patrols about the walls, tearing down houses to build engines of defence, rushing with his men from gate to battered gate, Harcla led the resistance with an energy and ingenuity to match all the Scots could level against him.

On the tenth day of the siege Bruce and Douglas adopted different tactics. Study of the fortifications had shown that one point on the west front appeared, because of the height of the walls and the difficulty of access, to be undefended. Douglas thought he could get a force up, and Robert therefore decided to employ the trick whereby Moray had gained Edinburgh Castle, himself launching the greater part of the army against the east wall in an assault fierce enough, it was hoped, to focus the entire attention of the defence, while Douglas 'with some others of the army who were most daring and nimble'* climbed the west wall to penetrate the town and take the defenders in the rear. Harcla, however, was not to be caught like that and Douglas, having managed to secure a bridgehead on the wall, met a resistance so vigorous as to dislodge him with heavy loss. A contributory cause of this failure may have been a wound suffered by Douglas himself; always ready to exploit the emotional dependence of soldiers on their leader by felling if he could the enemy captain, he could not prevent a like loss of morale in the Scots on his own disablement.

At this repulse Robert gave up, and the next day 'whether because they had heard the English were approaching to relieve the city or because they despaired of success, the Scots marched off in confusion to their own country, leaving behind them all their engines of war' (*Lanercost Chronicle*). The final seal was placed on their defeat when the pursuing English attacked and overcame their rearguard. This was altogether a poor year for the king and Douglas, who met with another setback a few months later, this time at Berwick where on the night of 14 January they mounted a surprise assault by land and sea. Moonlight revealed their approach, the garrison beat off both attacks, and Douglas himself escaped only with difficulty, in a small boat.

For Berwick's governor, Maurice of Berkeley, the frustration of this attempt was probably his sole satisfaction in a dreadful winter. Berwick was in dire case. The harvests had failed again in 1315, and famine was tightening its grip. Harsh enough in the countryside, this bore even more cruelly on townsfolk, dependent as they were on imports for much of their food.† There had been deaths by hunger in Berwick as early as October, when Berkeley wrote to King Edward that the garrison were threatening desertion unless the pay and victuals long promised them were supplied.

* *Lanercost Chronicle*.
† In Ypres, a town unaffected by war, the population fell by 5 per cent during the famine years 1314–17.

Something apparently was done, but by February whatever provisions had been sent had long been consumed, again starvation threatened, and the men-at-arms of the garrison—Gascons, most of them, from Edward's French duchy—demanded to be allowed to raid Scotland for food. Berkeley refused. His first duty was the defence of Berwick Castle, and he was well aware of the likely fate of raiders in Scotland. The Gascons retorted that it was better to die fighting than to starve. On St Valentine's Day more than eighty of them, led by one of their number called Raymond Cailhau, set out despite Berkeley's embargo to forage into Scotland.

They went up the Tweed almost as far as Melrose, and there divided into smaller groups to seize cattle, and peasants to herd the beasts back to Berwick. One of these parties went into the Merse and there, turning back with a spoil of beasts and prisoners, was observed by Adam of Gordon. Since Bannockburn Gordon had 'becomen Scottish man', and he at once sent word to Douglas of what he had seen. It did not occur to him that the men he had noted were not the only reivers abroad, nor did it to Douglas. Gordon's message was the first he had heard of the raid, and the numbers reported were no more than could conveniently be dealt with by the troops he had at hand and whatever support he could collect on the way. He set off with Sir Henry Balliol (probably Henry Balliol of Branksome in Selkirkshire) and Sir John Soules to catch the raiders before they could reach Berwick.

The Gascons meanwhile had recombined and set off down the Tweed with their spoil, and were on Scaithmoor, near Coldstream, by the time Douglas overhauled them. Hearing the sound of his pursuit, Cailhau had sent the prisoners and cattle on ahead and formed the Gascons into a schiltrom, and it was only on coming in sight of this ordered troop awaiting his attack that Douglas realized it was twice the size of the party reported to him, and twice that of his own force. An instant and unpleasant choice confronted him; either he must withdraw in face of the enemy, abandoning the people and the livestock it was his responsibility to defend, or take on a greatly superior force in open fight. Confidence in himself and his men, with a natural distaste for being seen to retreat, dictated the latter course. Commanding that his banner be unfurled in the recognized proclamation of intent to fight, he hurriedly drew up his men behind a ford, the only defensible feature within reach—the Gascons naturally were re-forming for attack, delighted to see how few they had to deal with—and cheerfully declared that the odds were heavy, but no heavier than he knew his men capable of overcoming. He was right, though he later confessed that he had never known harder fighting. The Scots at first were almost overwhelmed by the numbers against them and the fury of starving men fighting for food, and it was only when Douglas picked Cailhau out as the Gascons' leader and killed him that the tide turned; well aware how a captain's fall in battle could shake his soldiers' nerve, Douglas made it his policy to kill the enemy leader when he could as the quickest way to victory. So it proved here. The Scots prevailed, the prisoners and cattle were redeemed, and there returned to Berwick a handful out of the eighty-odd men who had defied Berkeley's veto. They may have been the unlucky ones all the same, for a month later Berkeley reported to Edward that the garrison were dying of hunger on the walls.

A few months after the Scaithmoor episode Douglas's responsibilities were greatly enlarged. In the summer of 1316 Moray returned from Ireland to report that the enterprise there was progressing so well that Edward Bruce, in sight of his crown at last, thought one strenuous effort more might suffice to establish the Scots' dominion in the island and that for this he asked reinforcements from Scotland, to be led by his brother in person. Robert acceded to this request. In September he left with Moray for Ireland, taking with him another contingent of soldiers (among them John Soules, who that summer had somewhat compensated for the defeat at Carlisle by capturing Andrew Harcla with much inferior numbers) and appointing as Wardens of Scotland in his absence his son-in-law the Steward and the lord of Douglas.

The actual powers and functions assigned the two wardens are unknown, as indeed is everything that might throw light on Douglas's civil activities. His military career, that alone interested contemporaries to the degree of recording it, must in fact have been only a part of his public life. The role allotted him in the later Regency Act is sufficient testimony to his competence in administration. It would indeed have been surprising had he failed in this; a clever, level-headed man, reared in the household of one of the time's most adroit statesmen, and a participant in politics no less than war since his majority, he must now at the age of thirty have been well equipped both by nature and by training for the tasks of government.

Whatever else might have been required of him as joint Warden of Scotland, Douglas saw that his chief concern must still be the Border, the more so as one likely effect of Robert's absence would be the emboldening of the English to fresh attack. It was probably for this reason that he now decided to build himself a new dwelling there. The location he chose was on the middle march, at the southern edge of his beloved Forest, where at Jedburgh the road descended from the English frontier at Carter Bar to meet Wheel Causey, the ancient road that traversed the Scottish borders from Annandale in the west to Roxburgh and Berwick in the east. From Jedburgh Douglas could cover any English descent by the middle approach, while a day's ride east or west would carry him to the other marches should danger threaten them. Jedburgh Castle had been surrendered to Robert soon after Bannockburn, and the town itself had been under Scottish control ever since, but the actual site Douglas chose lay two miles south, at Lintalee, where the hills shoulder in on either side of the Jed valley, squeezing between them the river and the road from England, while behind the western hill the Lintalee or Linthaugh burn on its way to join the Jed has cut a deep ravine. It was on the high platform of land between the Jed and the Lintalee that Douglas set workmen to building the manor and cnatonments from which he would command the Border.

The knowledge of King Robert's departure had its inevitable effect in England. In February 1317 Edward II appointed the earl of Arundel warden north of Trent, and Arundel, who had every intention of striking while the iron was hot and Scotland 'feeble of men', at once set about preparing a major descent upon the country. His plans appear to have entailed more than a raid, and possibly more than a single operation. His first aim was to demolish the forest of Jedburgh (for which purpose every soldier was issued with a felling-axe), as forming one of the natural strengths that constituted a serious hindrance to any would-be invader of Scotland. The Welsh had once used their great forests as the Scots did, as shelter from which to harry any invader, and Arundel's plan may have been based on Edward I's campaign against Llywellyn ap Gruffydd in 1277, which began with felling a great swathe of forest along the Flintshire coast through which the English army later advanced in safety to the conquest of Gwynedd. Arundel's felling excursion, whether or not the precursor to full invasion, itself entailed the use of a considerable force. Barbour declares that the English army on this occasion numbered ten thousand, while a contemporary English chronicler puts it at thirty thousand, and though even the lower figure is impossibly high it is plain that Arundel had gathered a far greater force than would have sufficed for a raid. His subordinate commanders included the earl of Atholl and Sir Henry Beaumont, while the chance survival of a claim for compensation for losses sustained on this expedition shows that one among the lesser knights present in unknown numbers was Sir William de Ros, who commanded fifty men-at-arms. The risks of meeting a prepared adversary were, moreover, diminished by a decision to move early in the year, before the English normally opened their campaigning season, and to enter Scotland by the desolate road over Carter Bar. Altogether Arundel's plans seem to have been well enough conceived and prepared to justify the confidence with which he adopted a line of advance along which, as he apparently knew, the Scottish Warden was likely to be found. He was in fact the only English commander who ever came near to catching Douglas napping.

Douglas was at Lintalee. His 'fair manor' was now complete, and he had decided by way of housewarming to give a feast there for his men. Famine was still raging to the south—in 1316 the harvest had failed for the third year running, and in England there were rumours of necrophagy, and worse—but Scotland appears to have been comparatively little affected, partly no doubt because the Lowlanders at least could supplement their diet with what little food the northern English could wrest from their sodden land, to have wrested from them by the Scots. In any case famine did not trouble the great, and Douglas had had no difficulty in purveying at Lintalee the wherewithal for a banquet. Preparations for it were well in hand when on 23 April word came to him that a great English army was well advanced towards the middle march.

As Arundel had probably reckoned, Douglas was not yet mobilized for the summer, having with him only his personal retinue. It numbered about two hundred men in all, fifty of them men-at-arms and the rest archers. With these, he at once decided, he must do what he could to frustrate the English. Lintalee he abandoned. The manor was fortified and could probably have been held awhile, but Douglas was not prepared to tie up any of his little force in the defence of an outpost which the English could probably invest with a fraction of their army. It was one of his strengths that he always kept his priorities clear, and he now unhesitatingly sacrificed his newly built manor to the primary objective of harassing and if possible halting the English advance.

A little south of Lintalee the road from England entered the Forest, running from the open into a great shield-shaped glade, wide towards England but narrowing northward till it was no more than a 'penny-stone-cast' across. In the neck of this glade a cleuch thick with young birch-trees cut in towards the roadside, and here Douglas stationed his archers. Before their position the birch saplings were plaited together into a screen firm enough to check a charge of cavalry but not so thick as to obscure their aim, and thus sheltered he left them with careful instructions when to loose fire and when to withdraw. The men-at-arms he led a little up the road, to a concealed position on its other side, and ambuscaded himself with them there to await the enemy.

The English vanguard was well into the narrowest part of the glade when he raised the cry of 'Douglas!' The hidden archers loosed a flight of arrows, and with his troopers Douglas burst from ambush, himself riding straight for the knight he had picked out as the English commander. This man, who wore a fur-edged hat over his helmet, responded bravely enough, spurring his own horse for Douglas, but the first shock of their encounter bore him to the ground and Douglas, pouncing down on him and whipping out a dagger, stabbed him to death. His men were now scattering the English vanguard all about the glade, while the archers poured their arrows into the next rank. Inequality of numbers precluded battle after the first surprise had had its effect; Douglas pulled the hat off the dead man's head, swung back into the saddle, called in his men and swept off into the Forest, to be rejoined there by the archers. The whole episode was over almost before the main English force realized anything had begun; a check ahead, a sudden hullabaloo from the glade, Douglas and his men tearing across their front to vanish again among the trees, then quiet, and the remnants of the vanguard staggering back towards them. Arundel, who had not expected such immediate confirmation of his theory about the Scottish forests, pulled back his army into the open and halted there while he considered what to do next. While he deliberated, Douglas was going into action again.

An English forage party led by a clerk called Ellis or Elias— the English chronicler calls him a 'noble schavaldur'*—had been moving parallel to and a little ahead of the main army on a line that brought them direct to Lintalee, where the manor stood deserted but not unwatched. There on taking possession they discovered with glee the food and wine laid in by Douglas for his housewarming. This was irresistible and they sat down at once to make the most of it, the knowledge that their involuntary host was the Black Douglas (whom they supposed to have fled before Arundel's overwhelming might) doubtless spicing their unexpected feast. They ate, drank and were merry, till the doors flew open and there loomed among them the mailed and towering Douglas backed by men fresh from killing and hot for more. The bill was now presented to the foragers, and for most of them it was their heads. One or two got away or were let escape to carry the news to Arundel, a few were taken prisoner for Douglas to question, the rest were put to the sword, and the housewarming of Lintalee ended with blood splashing the fresh plaster and soaking the green rushes on the floor. It was quickly over, and while some Scot of crude humour made the severed head of Ellis kiss his arse, Douglas, interrogating the prisoners, brought out the furred hat that was his trophy from the glade, showed it to them and asked if they knew whose it was. 'Richmond wears a hat like that', said one of them.

> Then Douglas blither was than ere:
> For he well wist that the Richmond,
> His deadly foe, was brought to ground.

His delight was in fact misplaced. The man he had killed was a Yorkshire knight called Thomas Richmond who had been leading the English vanguard and not, as Douglas supposed, John of

---

* The breakdown of order in northern England which resulted from Scottish raiding had given rise to widespread theft and rapine by native brigands, some of them well born; these malefactors, Gray tells us, were called schavaldurs, a term the derivation of which is obscure. Some of them were accused, probably with justice, of operating in conjunction with the Scots.

Brittany, earl of Richmond, whom both he and Robert seem to have detested.* His satisfaction at having as he thought killed the earl, however un-Christian, at least acquits him of rapacity; as a prisoner John of Brittany would have been worth £20,000 to him.

The next development seemed to confirm his understanding that he had killed the English commander-in-chief. Before he could even launch any further harassment against them the English turned tail and fled, leaving behind them what spoil they had gathered in their short advance into Scotland. Arundel had had enough. The Scottish use of their forests to damage invaders had been too thoroughly proved, their weakness in men, it seemed, wholly disproved; he must have gained the impression that a substantial force was operating against him. In due course word filtered south that the double repulse had been wholly achieved by Douglas with two hundred men. The Scotsman's reputation in England, already notable, now grew very great.

This among some Englishmen seems to have been for cunning even more than valour. If most of the English gentry saw in him 'the boldest and most enterprising knight in the two kingdoms',† to one chronicler at least he was 'James Douglas, always bent on plots'. This author‡ indeed equated Douglas with Achitophel, a curious judgment even from one to whom all Scots were traitors (to their rightful lord King Edward) since Douglas, who almost alone of the Scots nobility had never sworn fealty to an English king, was of all the Scottish captains least open to such a charge. Achitophel, however, was not merely a traitor but a promoter of treason in others, and the chronicler may have been moved by thoughts of Douglas's later activity in this respect. It could indeed be that as soon as he took up his wardenship he had begun to foment subversion in England. Warfare did not preclude intercourse across the border, this indeed being necessary in such matters as the negotiation and delivery of tribute and the ransoming of prisoners, in which Douglas as March Warden must have played an important part. It is likely that he used his English contacts as a source of intelligence, and entirely possible that he

* From Barbour's account of the rating Robert gave John of Brittany when he was captured at Byland in 1322, it appears that the king strongly resented something John had said; possibly Douglas did so too.
† Le Bel, presumably reporting here the opinion expressed to him by the English.   ‡ *Vita Edwardi Secundi.*

also took advantage of any chance he saw to subvert the potentially disaffected. 'This James of Douglas', observed Gray gloomily, 'was now very busy in Northumberland.' Without defining this 'busyness' Gray turns aside to deal, out of place, with the Soules conspiracy, but when he returns to Northumberland it is to record that a great part of the country had revolted against King Edward. The probability that Douglas was held—and indeed may have been—responsible for this accords well with the belief of some English chroniclers that the recapture of Berwick resulted from his bribes.* There may be some substratum of fact here. Douglas was sufficiently a realist to employ where appropriate undercover methods of advancing Scottish interests. It need not be inferred that he liked such tactics better than his colleagues did; by his office and his station near the Border he was better placed than they to discern and exploit opportunities of seducing Englishmen to Scottish ends.

Most Englishmen of the time, however, thought of Douglas solely in his military aspect. To the common folk of the north he was quite simply their ogre, most terrible of all the terrible Scots who yearly swept south to burn their homes, trample their crops and drive off their beasts, the Black Douglas who would get bad children. The gentry were inclined chiefly to admire him as preeminent in the one profession the noble held worthy of esteem, a supreme man of war. This admiration was not, however, universal, being emphatically unshared by Sir Robert Neville at least.

Neville, eldest son of the old lord of Raby and himself a man of some past distinction in the Scottish wars, known either from his taste in dress or from the obviousness of his self-esteem as the Peacock of the North, had lately found himself at odds with Sir Richard Marmeduke, lay steward to the bishopric of Durham, and at about this time† their rivalry culminated in a fight on the bridge

---

* The story in the *Brut* chronicle that Douglas bribed Harcla with 'a great deal of gold', though obviously a Lancastrian fabrication designed to twist against Harcla the rumour that Lancaster had taken a bribe from Bruce, also suggests that Douglas was looked on as the Scot most likely to suborn an Englishman.

† The date of Neville's encounters with Marmeduke and Douglas is uncertain. The one chronicler to date them (Bridlington) places the latter in June 1319, which can hardly be correct as both Barbour and Gray place it, by narrative detail as well as by sequence of events, before the recapture of Berwick.

at Durham (occasioned, Gray says, by a squabble as to which was the greater lord) in which Marmeduke was killed. This evoked King Edward's displeasure, and in the hope of regaining royal favour Neville resolved to undertake war service gratis, a decision that brought him, with a large and well-appointed train, to join the garrison at Berwick Castle. The regulars of this garrison were understandably among those who held Douglas in awe, and the Peacock soon found himself galled by constantly hearing the Scotsman's praise. One day, it seems, discussion turned on the unwisdom of engaging with Douglas, whereupon Neville burst out angrily that everyone talked as if there was nobody like Douglas, but if he, Neville, got the opportunity he would attack the Scot whatever they might say. Inevitably this conversation was reported to its subject, who said that Neville must be given his chance.

Turning out his troops, Douglas marched them down to Berwick by night, planted his banner in clear view of the castle and, to leave no doubt in what spirit he had come, dispatched some men to fire what buildings still survived in the vicinity. Daybreak revealed an unmistakable challenge. Before long the gates of the castle opened and Neville rode out, accompanied by his three younger brothers and backed by an imposing retinue. For all his brave words he appeared hesitant about assailing the Scotsman in his chosen position, and, evidently preferring defence to attack, stationed his troop on a nearby hill. Douglas waited until his fire-raisers rejoined him. By then he had satisfied himself that his troop could handle Neville's and, seeing no reason to attend the Peacock's convenience longer, marshalled his men and led them in a charge up the hill. Neville in turn swung his force into movement, and Scots and English crashed together on the slope. Through the immediate and fierce mêlée the two captains hacked a path towards each other until, 'where that the fighting fellest was', they met to plunge into the looked-for duel. It was no unequal combat, for Neville was a seasoned fighter who could deal blows as well as take them. Douglas, however, was the younger man and the more experienced soldier, and was moreover out to kill, while Neville almost certainly let himself be distracted, as indeed most knights of the day would have done, by the thought that Douglas taken alive would bring a luscious ransom. It was not long before he had underlined with his death the reputation he sought to challenge and Douglas, pleasantly breathed with his exertions, was yelling his battle-cry as he flung himself at the dismayed following of the Peacock. With their leader dead their resistance broke, and total rout speedily followed.

Douglas now decided that his own men, having been brought into action for his pleasure—and, as it turned out, profit—should have their chance of gain, and led them off on an impromptu raid all the spoil of which he gave them. He himself had done very well from his outing. Neville's folly in taking all his brothers with him into the fight almost ruined his family, for in his triumphant sweep through the defeated Englishmen Douglas had captured the lot—as well as 'the baron of Hilton', probably Sir Robert of Hilton in Durham—and the house of Raby had three ransoms to find at once. Ralph Neville, the Peacock's next brother, had to give Douglas hostages* and return home to try and raise the money; there survives a petition of his to King Edward begging aid and declaring that his father was reduced to alienating land to redeem his sons. The Peacock's end and the Nevilles' straits served as a warning to any other northern gentry who might dream of dealing with the Scots as the Scots now dealt with them.

> Sir James of Douglas in this wise,
> Through his worship and great emprise,
> Defended worthily the land.

From now on he had little occasion to do so with the sword. His reputation—his 'worship'—sufficed.

---

* One of these may have been his sister-in-law Ellen, the Peacock's widow, described as a prisoner in Scotland in 1320 when the countess of Fife was given a safe-conduct to fetch her home. If so, Ralph must by then have paid off his own ransom at least.

Chapter 7

Sorts of Traitors

> Duties to kings they be conditional.
> Fulke Greville

Towards the end of March 1318, Douglas received from the king a command to attend in Duns Park, Berwickshire, on 1 April with a small troop of soldiers equipped for battle. Obeying, he found there, likewise accompanied, the earl of Moray and Robert Keith the Marischal. It was Keith who explained their summons.

Among his connections by marriage Keith numbered one Peter, or Sim, of Spalding, who was a burgess of Berwick. The defence of this town had the previous year been among the economies decided on by Edward II as a means of retrenchment without inconvenience to himself or his favourites; ceasing to maintain a professional garrison there additional to that in the castle, he entrusted the keeping of the town to its burgesses. The measure was ill-judged, for the people of Berwick were not especially well disposed to his rule, and the arrogant conduct of the castle's new governor, Roger Horsley, did nothing to sweeten it to them. Spalding at least felt King Robert would be preferable, and accordingly wrote to his kinsman telling him Berwick was ripe for conquest, and that if on the night of 1 April Keith brought troops to the Cowgate, where Spalding would be on guard duty, they would be admitted. This letter cast the Marischal into great uncertainty. Leaving aside the question whether Spalding could be trusted, his own insufficiency of resources for such a task necessitated the choice, which he felt beyond him, of a leader for the enterprise. A further complication was that the Pope had recently attempted to impose a truce on the English and the Scots, and even though Robert had not acceded to it the recapture of Berwick at this time might be ill received by him. After mulling the whole thing over for a while Keith took his letter and his doubts to the king. Robert decided at once that the letter must be acted on. As to the other matter, he said, Keith had done rightly; if he had called in either of the two obvious men for the job, Moray or Douglas, the other would have resented it. Moray, garlanded with fresh laurels from Ireland, had returned to Scotland with Robert the previous year, leaving Edward Bruce wearing the longed-for crown but still fighting for the kingdom that went with it. Clearly the earl and Douglas still felt a mutual emulousness in achievement of which Robert was aware. That he knew too that their friendship was never darkened by this rivalry is suggested by his solution of Keith's problem. Douglas and Moray should share the enterprise.

His judgment had been right; the two commanders were perfectly willing to co-operate. Having digested Keith's report and agreed on a plan of operation, they set off at once for the Cowgate. Spalding's offer had been genuine. He was waiting there and kept watch as ladders were set up on the wall and the Scots ascended. Soon all were within, and the two commanders set quietly about their preparations. Instead of precipitating night fighting in narrow streets to which their men were strangers, they planned to effect a quick and as nearly as possible bloodless takeover at dawn, and with this in mind distributed the greater part of their company in small groups about the town to await the call to action, while they themselves, attended only by their personal suites, took up a position by the wall. Their plan, however, assumed a firmer discipline than they could rely on. For some of the men-at-arms scattered waiting among the dark buildings, unwatched by their officers, the thought of a city's loot grew gradually irresistible. Temptation overcoming them, they began to break into the sleeping houses, and the townsfolk jerked awake to the knowledge that invaders were in their midst. All chance of a quick, systematic takeover vanished as unplanned fighting erupted now in one place and now another, and dawn broke on a score of disorganized combats as the townsmen seized weapons and rushed out to tackle Scots whose greed had scattered them beyond quick recombination.

By now the alert had reached the castle. Horsley might have made himself unpopular in Berwick, but he was a brave soldier and a quick-witted one. Realizing that there was still time to save the town, he whipped the garrison to arms, dashed out speedily enough to cut off Douglas and Moray from their disordered troops and, with a sense of priorities to match Douglas's own, made straight for the two isolated leaders. Their small retinues much outnumbered by the garrison troop, they were very near to being overcome, and Horsley's failure to win the glory of capturing Robert's two greatest generals was due very largely to the wits and energy of young William Keith of Galston, the Marischal's newly knighted cousin, who managed to sweep up as many of the Scots as were near him and with them slashed a way through to the Cowgate to take Horsley in flank. With this reinforcement Douglas and Moray drove him back, failing nevertheless to cut him off from the castle; regaining it in safety with his men, he barred the gates and made ready for defence, while outside the capture of the town at last began to go according to plan. The two commanders got their men in hand again, checking any attacks on people who made no resistance, and soon could send word to Robert that the last portion of his kingdom awaited his entry.

Douglas, normally calm in victory and defeat alike, blazed with joy as he rode through Berwick, declaring that entrance into Paradise itself could gladden him no more. After twenty-two years the son had redeemed the father's failure, and Berwick was Scottish again. All the same, Horsley held out eleven weeks in the castle Sir William had surrendered in a day.

While with diminishing hope of relief he defended the castle, those Scots not engaged in its siege drove once more into Northumberland for a brief and triumphant campaign that brought them the castles of Wark, Harbottle and Mitford, and kept on southward as far as Knaresborough, burning Northallerton and Boroughbridge and exacting £1,000 protection money from Ripon before turning home again. In the whole of Northumberland now only the town of Newcastle and the castles of Bamburgh, Alnwick and Norham remained to Edward; and even Bamburgh and Alnwick were treating with the Scots, said the son of Norham's then constable, the chronicler Gray.*

* Gray, and the English chronicler quoted in Stevenson's *Illustrations of Scottish History*, attribute Spalding's action to a bribe from Douglas and go on to say that, reward being withheld, Spalding turned against Robert

By a felicitous chance the year of Berwick's recapture also witnessed the completion after 150 years of the cathedral of St Andrews. On 5 July King Robert, with a great assembly of lords spiritual and temporal, attended the dedication of the building. Douglas can hardly have been absent from a ceremony at once so significant nationally and of such importance to his boyhood's protector. Since making his way back to Scotland from prison bishop Lamberton had continued his extraordinary career as a diplomat so skilful as openly to serve two warring masters. In the abortive peace negotiations of 1310 he had been one of Edward's representatives, and in 1313 he acted as English envoy in France. Yet all the while he had been active in Scotland, where his heart lay, and where despite his involvement in politics he continued to show himself a conscientious bishop to his see. His episcopate, notable for the building of ten new churches, was crowned by the cathedral's completion, and it must have been one of the happiest days of his life when he consecrated the great church before a congregation headed by a king of Scotland who at last ruled the entire realm of Alexander III.

A less pleasing ecclesiastical ceremony was now impending. The previous year Pope John XXII had attempted to impose a two-year truce on England and Scotland. Robert, giving the papal envoys unwilling but courteous audience, felt little filial obedience to an intermediary plainly neutral on Edward's side—John's partiality had been manifest from the start in his refusal to address the king by his royal title—and had not felt himself precluded by papal decree from recapturing Berwick. Pope John, however, choosing to regard this as a violation of a truce to which Scotland had never subscribed, and further irritated by the abuse of another papal envoy, who had been turned back at Berwick because the missive he bore was not directed to the King of Scots and robbed by a notorious English 'schavaldur' as he returned through the Northumbrian waste, now pronounced a fresh sentence of excommunication on Robert Bruce,* his kindred, adherents,

---

and was executed. The latter part of the story is incorrect (it may derive from the fate of Piers Lubeaud, once Edward's governor of Edinburgh), for Robert rewarded Spalding with estates in Angus, and this casts doubts on the first. Possibly Douglas had been negotiating separately with another townsman, who unsuccessfully tried to cash in on Spalding's act.
* He had of course already been excommunicated after Comyn's murder.

counsellors and supporters, and laid Scotland under an interdict. His bulls were naturally welcomed in England and made the most of there, the sentence pronounced thrice at mass in every church anathematizing not merely Robert's adherents in general but, by name with the king himself, Thomas Randolph, earl of Moray, and James, lord of Douglas. But the people who should have been most affected remained unmoved (*Lanercost Chronicle*): 'the Scots stubbornly pertinacious, cared nothing for any excommunication, nor would they pay the slightest attention to the interdict'. As for Douglas, if his personal excommunication moved any response in him, it was probably one of gratification that south of the border he was reckoned one of the three most important men in Scotland. This back-handed accolade was soon followed by a far greater one at home.

On 14 October the Scottish kingdom in Ireland received its deathblow when Edward Bruce came characteristically to his end. Faced at Dundalk with an English army greatly outnumbering his own, rejecting with contempt all counsel to avoid battle till the disparity was reduced by the arrival of reinforcements known to be only a day or so distant, he insisted on fighting at once, and was defeated and killed together with all those who had advised against battle. They included Philip Mowbray, the Steward's younger brother John, and John Soules, the knight who had captured Andrew Harcla in Eskdale. Edward Bruce's death threw the Scottish succession into doubt once more. He himself left only bastards, while Robert's sole legitimate issue was his two-year-old grandson Robert Stewart, the only child of Marjorie Bruce, who had died in 1316. At Scone on 3 December a fresh Act of Succession settled the crown, in default of a male heir of the king's body, on this child, much later to reign as Robert II. The Act continued:

> The lord king, with the unanimous consent of one and all of the community, has assigned the wardship and care of the said Robert, or of other heir lawfully begotten of the body of the lord King, together with the custody of the whole Kingdom and people, if at the time of the decease of the lord King the heir shall be of minor age, to the noble man Lord Thomas Randolph, earl of Moray and lord of Man, and if in the meantime the said earl shall have chanced to die, to the noble man James, Lord of Douglas.

Moray was the obvious choice as regent-designate; a man of proven ability, he was also the only surviving adult male of the king's blood, and high in rank. Considerations of this kind, which normally predominated in the mediaeval mind, would have suggested as regent in reserve either one of the king's brothers-in-law or, even more strongly, the Steward, father of the heir presumptive. The nomination and the acceptance of Douglas were a rare salute to merit.

The loss of Berwick, last English holding in Scotland, had moved even Edward II to bellicosity, and by 1319 he was well placed to attempt a riposte. The earl of Pembroke, the one English magnate of the time whose conduct suggests an awareness of the obligations as well as the privileges of rank, had managed to patch up the worst differences between king and magnates, and it was with as little disharmony as the reign had ever experienced that Edward and his baronage concerted plans for the recovery of Berwick. Even earl Thomas of Lancaster, greatest and most obstreperous of Edward's opponents, now joined for the first time in an expedition against Scotland, making one of six earls who came to the great muster Edward held at Newcastle in July. Thence the army headed north, its movement paralleled by that of the ships that were to assail the town by sea, to reach Scotland on 29 August. Berwick was ready for them. Robert, having provisioned and munitioned it in full, had committed its defence to the Steward, who had not only garrisoned the town with the men of his following and with such specialized troops as archers and crossbowmen, but laid on the ablest engineer he could find to purvey and supervise the use of engines of defence.

In the fields about the town on its land side the English pitched their tents,

> So many, they a town made there
> More than both town and castle were.

Beyond, they dug entrenchments and threw up ramparts to defend this camp against any relieving army. At sea the ships of their fleet closed up the harbour entrance. Six days passed in thus sealing off the invested town and on 7 September assault began by land and sea. It was energetically mounted—and as energetically repelled by the defenders under the Steward—but in the mind of every English leader was the thought that it was essentially a forcing bid. The siege of Berwick was a challenge Robert could not ignore. An army must be sent to relieve the threatened town, and when it got there Bannockburn would be avenged.

Robert had every intention of relieving Berwick, and none of engaging a prepared English army in open field. An army had been mobilized under the joint command of Moray and Douglas, and this he sent not eastward toward Berwick but south into England with instructions to 'burn and slay', harrying the land till Berwick's assailants raised the siege in fear for their own homes. They entered by Carlisle and drove southward, 'leaving behind', in Trokelowe's words, 'ashes, cinders, the fumes of smoke and slain bodies unburied in every town they passed', as far as the North Riding. There Edward's queen, Isabelle of France, was staying, at Boroughbridge, to await her husband's return from the capture of Berwick, and this suggested to Douglas a new means of casting the English into dismay. What happened next is best told from the English side (*Vita Edwardi Secundi*).

> One day a certain spy was captured at York, and when he saw that he would be put to the question he promised, if he should be allowed to forego that penalty, to betray the whole conspiracy of the Scots; this pact was agreeable to the citizens. The Archbishop of York and the King's chancellor at that time, the bishop of Ely, were there too. The spy then explained that our enemy James Douglas was to come to these parts secretly with his chosen band, to abduct the queen and also kill all those whom he should take unawares. 'They were lying hidden', he said, 'on such a day and in such a place, and at the appropriate moment would carry out their project.' Hardly anyone believed this story, because the lord King of England had already begun to lay waste the lands of the Scots, and it appeared more necessary for such an army (as that of the Scots) to defend its own frontier than to seek battle a hundred miles outside its own territory. But the spy added that if he were not justified by events he would willingly submit to capital punishment.
>
> Then the archbishop and the chancellor went forth from the city with their usual retinues, the sheriff and the burgesses and their followers, the monks and canons and other regulars,

as well as anyone else who could handle a weapon, and brought the queen back into the city; thence she was taken by water to Nottingham. That was a safer place for the queen, where neither James nor his traps were to be feared.

Archbishop Melton then set about tackling the invaders as best he might in the absence at Berwick of almost all the fighting men of the county. The townsmen of York, militia trained to handle weapons in defence of their walls but quite unaccustomed to fighting in the open, turned out under their mayor, priests and peasants took up arms, the archbishop's silver crucifix was brought out as a standard, and on 20 September Melton and Hotham of Ely led out this pathetic host to face the most experienced professional soldiers in Europe. The 'spy' had said the Scots were to be found across the Swale, near Myton, and thither Melton led his amateur army. Beyond the river smoke was rising, and once across the Englishmen found it blowing in their faces; the Scots, finding some stacks of damp hay, had provided themselves with a smokescreen. Struggling through with streaming eyes, the English saw the Scots their 'spy' had promised them, not scattered and unsuspicious, but drawn up in schiltrom to await their coming. As the unaccustomed warriors wavered towards them the Scots let out a yell so fearful as to quench all heart for battle. The unhappy Englishmen turned and fled in wild disorder, while their trained and officered enemy at once reorganized for pursuit, the hobelars swinging to horse and cutting off the English retreat to the bridge, while the foot-soldiers drove them back against the river. Melton and Hotham got away—as did Melton's standard-bearer, swimming the river with the silver crucifix which, before the archbishop got it back, was to undergo strange adventures including concealment in a peasant's thatch—but William Ayreminne, Edward's Keeper of the Rolls, was taken prisoner, and the mayor of York was killed. With him died many of his burgesses, 'Swale drowning more than the sword killed', and of the clerics who had followed their archbishop to war so many that the Scots called the affair, hardly to be dignified with the name of battle, the Chapter of Myton.

The author of *Vita Edwardi Secundi*, recording this débâcle, could find only one comfort: the queen had been saved. Evidently he had failed, certain though he was of Douglas's cunning, fully to plumb its depths. It is unlikely that Douglas had ever hoped to capture Isabelle. As the Scots were not equipped, and had not the time, to undertake a siege, she had only to get inside walls to be safe. His aim had been to raise, with the aid of planted information, a tocsin loud enough to call the English from the siege of Berwick. In this the Scots had largely succeeded even before the news of Myton reached Edward. The first report of their movements came to him on 14 September, on the morrow of a fierce but unsuccessful assault on the town. The news that a Scottish army was ravaging the north of England unopposed spread instant division among the besiegers. The knights and nobles whose homes lay in the north demanded that the siege be broken off and the army move to meet and destroy the Scots, while the southerners insisted that Berwick could not hold out much longer, and the siege must be pressed to its conclusion. Edward upheld this view, but Lancaster took the northerners' part, threatening to withdraw his own forces, and as these made up an appreciable segment of the English army, the threat was not one to be lightly brushed aside. The news of Myton settled the matter, and on 24 September the English broke camp. Their only hope of satisfaction now was to catch and destroy the returning Scots. To reduce their chance of unopposed passage, Edward and Lancaster divided, Edward going south by the east march and Lancaster by the west; and the Scots, pursuing their incendiary way northward by Wharfedale, Craven and Gilsland, slid between them and safely home.

This affair seriously damaged Lancaster's good name. As the centre of opposition to an unpopular king he had long enjoyed public favour incommensurate with his deserts, while his abstention from previous expeditions against Scotland had preserved him from any share in the discredit resulting from their failure. He was now associated not only with a failure but with one arguably attributable to his conduct. From that attribution it was only a step to the suspicion that his actions had been interested. Stories began to fly about the country that Lancaster had had a secret understanding with Bruce; that he had received a bribe of £40,000 from the Scottish king; that his complicity was proved by his failure to intercept and defeat the returning Douglas. Lancaster was sufficiently offended by these rumours to insist on clearing himself by compurgation, but they may have sown in his mind, as the prohibition of unthought-of mischief in a child's, possibilities to germinate later action.

It was a great good fortune to Scotland at this time that, while the government of England was jerked along by a pack of squabbling nincompoops, the handful of highly talented individuals who directed Scottish affairs worked together in a harmony remarkable in any mediaeval realm and extraordinary in one later notorious for faction. This was particularly exemplified in the partnership of Douglas and Moray. Joint military command was then a fairly usual expedient. It derived from the nature of mediaeval armies, which still tended to be less single organizations than *ad hoc* federations of small armies individually led; failing the unquestionable authority of a monarch as commander-in-chief, these had often to be jointly steered by the leaders of their components. The independence that necessitated this expedient could naturally give rise to fresh complications, and the association of Douglas and Moray was potentially subject to a further risk in that the lesser in rank of the two, and hence in the last resort the subordinate, was the abler—and far the more unorthodox—soldier. That the partnership functioned so smoothly none the less is much to Moray's credit. From Barbour's account of the one jointly commanded expedition to be described in detail,* it appears that Moray not only left to Douglas the actual management of the army (which probably appealed less to him anyway than it did to his professionally-minded colleague) but was the ultimate yielder in any disagreement over strategy. It is true that Douglas was now generally recognized as, after Robert, the finest soldier of the day, but Moray himself was a commander of distinction, and for him not only to share that view but act on it argues real magnanimity.

The English had not seen the last for that year of the terrible pair (*Lanercost Chronicle*).

> The excommunicate Scots, not satisfied with the aforesaid misdeeds, invaded England with an army commanded by the aforesaid two leaders, to wit, Thomas Randolph and James of Douglas, about the feast of All Saints, when the crop had been

---

* The Weardale campaign of 1327. There is no reason to suppose this atypical. English references to their joint operations and Le Bel's account of the Weardale campaign bear out Barbour's picture of Douglas as the dominant partner.

stored in barns, and burned the whole of Gilsland, both the corn upon which the people depended for sustenance during that year and the houses wherein they had been able to take refuge; also, they carried off with them both men and cattle. And so, marching as far as Borough under Stanemoor, they laid all waste, and then returned through Westmorland, doing there as they had done in Gilsland, or worse. Then after ten or twelve days they fared through part of Cumberland, which they burned on their march, and returned to Scotland with a very large spoil of men and cattle.

When a month later Edward sought and Robert conceded a truce, the English observed bitterly that the Scots were less fatigued with war than glutted with spoil.*

The truce came into force at the end of December, to endure for two years. This measure did not in Edward's view render it incumbent on him to cease seeking his enemy's harm by non-violent means, and he was much satisfied when his continued pressure on Pope John for further commination of the Scots was rewarded by the issue of fresh bulls of excommunication, with a requirement for continual renewal of the sentence till Robert should make amends to Edward. This sentence did evoke response in Scotland, but not of a kind either Edward or the Pope had bargained for. Aided by the clergy or at least by Robert's chancellor Bernard Linton, who probably acted as their draftsman, eight earls led by Fife, the premier earl, and Moray, the officers of state, twenty-seven barons and knights led by Douglas and 'the whole community of the realm of Scotland' issued on 6 April 1320 the manifesto known as the Declaration of Arbroath.

Opening with the legendary, then firmly credited, migrations of their ancestors from Scythia to Spain by way of the Tyrrhenian Sea, they related the winning, by victory after victory, of the abodes in the west which now they held, and had kept,

> evermore free from any servitude. . . . Until the magnificent prince Edward, King of the English, father of him who reigns now, came in the guise of a friend and ally with a hostile intent against our realm when it lacked a head,

* Gray wrote of the period after the recapture of Berwick that 'the Scots had got so completely the upper hand and were so insolent that they held the English to be of almost no account'.

SORTS OF TRAITORS

against a people who had no thought of ill or fraud, unused to the assaults of war. The wrongs he did among them, slaughter, violence, pillage, burning, prelates imprisoned, monasteries given to the flames, the inmates despoiled and slain, and these not all his lawless deeds, sparing neither age, sex, order of religion or priesthood, only he who saw and suffered might recount or comprehend.

From these unnumbered ills, with the aid of Him who heals the wounded and makes whole, we have been delivered by the strong arm of our prince and king, our lord Sir Robert who, that he might free his people and his heritage from the hands of foes, a second Maccabaeus as it were or a Joshua, cheerfully endured toil and weariness, hunger and peril. And he it is that by the providence of God, by rightful succession after our laws and customs, the which we will maintain even unto death, and by the dutiful consent and assent of every one of us, has been made our prince and king. Unto him, as the man through whom salvation has been wrought in our people, we are bound both of right and by his service rendered, and are resolved in whatever fortune to cleave, for the preservation of our liberty. Were he to abandon the enterprise begun, choosing to subject us or our kingdom to the King of the English or to the English people, we would strive to thrust him out forthwith as our enemy and the subverter of right, his own and ours, and take for our king another who would suffice for our defence, for so long as an hundred remain alive we are minded never a whit to bow beneath the yoke of English dominion. It is not for glory, riches or honour that we fight; it is for liberty alone, that no good man relinquishes but with his life.

And now, carrying the spiritual war magnificently into the enemy's country, they warned Pope John to look to his own soul, for 'if your Holiness take us not at our word, all the evil to be done by them [the English] in us and by us in them we believe the Almighty must lay to your account'.

This powerful defiance, though it did not secure the lifting of the papal sentence, did startle the Pope into suspending further action against Robert and into writing privately to Edward urging him to consider the possibility of making peace with the

Scots. Edward was always ready to consider this on his own terms, and in September appointed commissioners to treat for peace. The negotiations failed, no doubt on the usual grounds, and in November Edward was instructing the earl of Atholl, the Northumbrian earl of Angus and Andrew Harcla to admit to the King of England's peace, as secretly as they could, such Scots as felt their consciences troubled by the excommunication. This seems to have been not without effect, for early in 1321 Atholl reported that Sir Alexander Mowbray and several other Scotsmen had come to England and wished to be received. The English court must also have been gratified to learn later that year of the secret plans of a group of Scottish nobles to assassinate Robert and place lord Soules on the throne,* a project which by one account was first disclosed to King Robert by a Scotsman who at about this time transferred his allegiance from Edward to Robert. Edward had little time, however, to rejoice in the knowledge that there still remained some pockets of disaffection in Scotland. His own realm was once again racked with faction, and Atholl had not long counted up his tiddlers when Douglas found himself playing a whale. Before the year was out Douglas was in correspondence with Thomas, earl of Lancaster.

England's misfortunes at this time included not only a head of state who was both lazy and stupid, but a leader of the opposition to match. That Thomas of Lancaster should head the baronial resistance to Edward II was inevitable. The son of an English prince by a former Queen of Navarre, the King of England's cousin, uncle to the King of France and the Queen of England, lord of three earldoms in his own right and two in his wife's, in his own eyes plainly entitled to a unique authority in the state, he was the ineluctable leader of any faction opposing a king who cared to give such authority to his minions alone. Only when Edward's discrediting at Bannockburn permitted Thomas to grasp the power he felt rightly his were his supporters enabled to judge his capacity to wield it. Thomas, however, besides being handicapped by a rebarbative personality and by the inability to compensate for it by using the patronage with which Edward could at least buy supporters, was little more inclined to business

* Their plans presumably entailed the disposal also of Moray, Douglas and the Steward, who could hardly have been expected to stand by while Robert's assassin usurped his grandson's heritage.

than his cousin, while his period of authority coincided both with the start of the famine years and with the worsening of Scottish depredations. Within a year or two the suspicion that King Log had been exchanged for earl Log had enabled Pembroke to build up a group of moderates and isolate Lancaster. But Lancaster's gift for disillusioning his adherents was excelled by Edward's for making enemies through his favourites. Already at the siege of Berwick a new star had been rising in the royal household, and by 1320 Hugh Despenser's dominance of the king and government of England was complete.

Despenser, a clever man and a capable administrator, might have proved worthy of his power had he not been greedy to a degree that shocked even a rapacious age. Thorough and efficient in his acquisitiveness as in his rule, he was as ready to screw ten pounds out of a bishop for admission to temporalities lawfully due as to scheme the ousting of his brothers-in-law from their wives' inheritance. No man could feel safe in his property while Despenser ran the country, least of all those to whom he was neighbour. By 1320 the moderates were reduced to impotence and men were looking to Lancaster, who had destroyed Gaveston, as the only man who might bring Despenser down. By the end of that year Despenser's prevention of a sale of land in Gower, obviously designed to lead to forfeiture in his interest, had rallied against him every nobleman of the Welsh March. In a Parliament at Westminster in July 1321, the earl of Hereford, Roger Mortimer of Chirk and his nephew Mortimer of Wigmore, backed by the other marcher lords and with the tacit support of the absent Lancaster, managed to impose on Edward his favourite's banishment. Experience with Gaveston had, however, taught the English barons that it was easier to get a favourite exiled than to keep him away. The atmosphere remained inflammable, and in October a match was struck. Queen Isabelle, travelling to Canterbury, went to the royal castle of Leeds in Kent, whose constable, Badlesmere, belonged to the opposition. He was absent, but his wife refused the queen admission and forcibly resisted an attempt at entry, killing half a dozen of the queen's entourage. This outrage swung moderate opinion back to Edward's side, and a substantial force was soon at his disposal. By the end of the month Leeds was captured, and Edward plainly planning the use of this army to deal with the hostile barons. Hereford and the Mortimers were already in arms, but they hesitated to move without Lancaster's aid, and the earl, who had a private quarrel with Badlesmere, still seemed disinclined for any action beyond calling one of the personal 'parliaments' of his Midland adherents with which he liked to titillate his self-importance. Even Lancaster, however, could not fail to realize that a crisis was impending, and it cannot have been long after the fall of Leeds that he made contact with Douglas. The first evidence of their correspondence is a safe-conduct for Lancaster's agent Richard Topcliff, issued by Douglas on 6 December.

Lancaster was of course too big a fish for Douglas to play alone, and the king and Moray were probably brought into the matter at once. Robert appears to have acquiesced rather than participated in the negotiations that now began, and it was the younger men who, reasoning no doubt that what was bad for Edward was good for Scotland, went ahead with beguiling the earl further into treason. This did not, however, deter them from re-opening hostilities as soon as the truce expired. On 6 January they were over the border, accompanied this time by the Steward, for a fortnight's systematic plundering of the half-recovered north. Moray posted himself at Darlington while Douglas ranged eastward toward Hartlepool and south almost as far as the Cleveland Hills, and the Steward down to Richmond where the people, 'neither having nor hoping to have any defender',* bought him off with the usual tribute. The northern gentry, meanwhile, appalled at the prospect of seeing the sufferings their homelands had undergone before the truce indefinitely renewed, and despairing of help from the king, had gone to Lancaster at his castle at Pontefract and begged him to lead them against the Scots. One of their number, however, was not with them. The loyal and honourable Harcla had correctly gone to Edward to beg that he come to the defence of the north. To him Edward answered that the rebellion in England must first be put down, and Harcla returned home convinced that the disposal of Lancaster and his confederates was a prerequisite to the conquest of the Scots. Lancaster, meanwhile, had been returning a cognate answer to his petitioners; he would not take up arms in the cause of a king who was making ready to attack him. The disappointed northerners, returning to their pillaged homes, must have passed Richard

* *Lanercost Chronicle*.

Topcliff as he headed for Pontefract from a conference with Moray and Douglas at Corbridge.

But Lancaster's inertia had already lost the moment for effective action. Supported by the earls of Pembroke, Richmond and Surrey, Edward had early in January advanced on the marcher lords. The two Mortimers, having vainly waited for Lancaster to join them, surrendered to him on 22 January and were sent to the Tower, while Hereford with the lesser rebels fled north to their torpid ally and there joined in his treatings with the Scots. These were now so far advanced that a meeting to settle the terms of agreement was feasible. On 16 February Moray issued a safe-conduct for Robert lord Clifford (son of the one-time temporary lord of Douglas), John Mowbray and their entourage, these two apparently being the emissaries of the English rebels, and a day or two later Lancaster's messenger left Scotland for his lord with the following letter from Douglas*—addressed to 'King Arthur', a sobriquet presumably chosen to flatter Lancaster's self-esteem:

> Greetings as to himself. Sire, know that the bearer of these came where he thought to have found us on the 7th day of February, but he did not find us there, wherefore he could not be answered as to the business before the 17th day of February for a certain reason, which he will tell you; and we have sent the letter of conduct by him. And in regard to the place where the conference may best be held, the bearer of these will tell you by word of mouth what seems good to us; and if it may please you to come to that place, or otherwise where it seems good to you, let us know six days previously. Adieu.

This letter suggests that its composer was no novice in clandestine correspondence. From its contents nothing could be learned but that an unnamed person was communicating with Douglas, and at an unidentified place likely to meet him—an encounter for which there could be, even in time of war, legitimate reason. Douglas could hardly have drafted his letter more carefully had he foreseen its ultimate fate, which was to fall into the hands of Edward's officers. By then it would be the least of the evidence against Lancaster.

* Written, like the safe-conducts and the letter to Neville, in Norman French.

The conference took place, resulting in the production of an agreement whereby Moray and Douglas—and, nominally, Robert—undertook, without claiming any territorial concession, to aid to the best of their power the earls of Lancaster and Hereford and their allies against their enemies in England, Wales and Ireland, and Lancaster and Hereford in return promised, when their quarrel was settled, to do all in their power to bring about a lasting peace between England and Scotland. The moderation of the return the Scots required indicates that the Declaration of Arbroath had spoken no more than the truth in stating that they fought only for their liberty. The matter settled, Lancaster marched south to confront his cousin, while on the Border Douglas and Moray awaited the summons to join him.

Douglas may at this time have been trying to inveigle into support of Lancaster some of the Englishmen with whom he was in touch. There survives among the documents concerning Lancaster's rebellion a copy of a brief and apparently hasty letter of his to his former captive Ralph Neville. 'For any business that concerns us', he wrote, 'I pray you send me Richard Thirlwall, as speedily as you can, for he has safe-conduct; and if he cannot come send me any other sure man who can certify you as to what shall be done in the matters that concern us.' In Neville's case, Douglas's caginess of style paid off; Neville emerged unscathed, having evidently satisfied the royal officers that 'the matters that concern us' were permissible business. So indeed they may have been, though if so it is difficult to see why Douglas should not have specified them openly.

By 8 March Lancaster was at Burton, preparing to meet the royal army advancing from the south. As it passed Lichfield he came out to give battle, then suddenly lost heart, turned and fled. At Tutbury he briefly paused, then headed on north, his cousin in hot pursuit. While Lancaster fled northwards and his allies awaited the unsent summons, the levies of Westmorland, led by Sir Andrew Harcla, were on their way south. On 16 March Lancaster's army reached Boroughbridge to find Harcla already there, holding the Ure crossing against them, with men drawn up on foot in schiltrom formation and archers on their wings in support in the first known use of the disposition that was to win Crécy and Poitiers. In an attempt to force the bridge Hereford was killed; a copy of the treaty with the Scots was later found in his baggage. Lancaster, seeking and obtaining a truce till the next day, failed to put it to its one possible use, flight to Scotland, and the next morning, his retreat cut off by the Yorkshire levies, surrendered. On 19 March Edward at last avenged Gaveston. Brought to trial in his own hall at Pontefract, denied the right to speak in self-defence as Gaveston had been denied it, the great earl was condemned as a traitor and led out to a nearby hill to have his head struck off as Gaveston's had been. His death was followed by extensive proscriptions among his allies and followers. Some twenty-five barons and knights suffered the extreme penalty of treason, many of them northerners who had turned to Lancaster out of despair at Edward's neglect of their defence.

Edward at last had won a victory, and even if it was over his own subjects and gained by no prowess of his own, it had put him in a winning mood. He was mindful too of his promise to Harcla —now, in recognition of his services at Boroughbridge, created earl of Carlisle. The executions were hardly finished before preparations began for a fresh invasion of Scotland, 13 June being set for the muster at Newcastle. By that date Edward was far from ready to take the field, and Robert fully prepared. On 17 June the King of Scots marched by way of Westmorland south to waste the country as far as Furness, thence crossing the sands of Morecambe Bay to burn Lancaster, where Moray and Douglas joined him for a sweep as far south as Preston. Altogether the Scots and their king enjoyed a month's unimpeded devastation of north-west England before returning home to make ready for the invasion of their own country.

Robert was not so bold as to demand from heaven a repetition of the grace that had granted Bannockburn. Unlike that of 1314, this invasion of Edward's was not the outcome of a Scottish invitation, and there was nothing discreditable in a reversion to his old strategy of eschewing battle. This he now carried to its extremest degree yet, stopping only at the actual burning of the land. As far as possible all that went on foot was taken north out of Lothian, as was much of what could be carried, so that when at the beginning of August Edward at last advanced into Scotland, Robert and the main Scottish army withdrawing into Fife and Douglas into the Forest, the English, taking the coastal road 'to do more damage', met neither man nor beast.

Halted at Edinburgh, they found themselves in a desert. There was no sign of the Scottish king or his army, nor were any people to be found from whom news of his movements might be wrung. There were no cattle or sheep on the pastures, no crops in the barns, no chickens in the empty villages. Forage parties returned empty-handed, all but one that found one lame cow in a field at Tranent; the earl of Surrey said sourly that it was the dearest beef he had ever seen. This dearth should not have been a serious matter, for the English had never reckoned on living off the country and supply ships had been dispatched to meet Edward at Edinburgh, but the very weather now turned Scot and contrary winds held them outside the Forth. The food that could be harvested from the empty country was too little by far to feed as many as were gathered at Edinburgh. Hunger sharpened into famine, dysentery followed, and it was soon plain even to Edward that he must either retreat or see his army disintegrate without battle from sickness and starvation. Towards the end of the month the English turned homeward, trailed unawares by Douglas as they laboured down the road along the eastern edge of the Forest.

As the main army plodded through Lauderdale their light horsemen, hopeful of better success in new terrain, went ahead to forage and to bivouac at Melrose Abbey. Douglas, however, guessed their destination and was there first, ambushing his troops near the gate and posting 'a right sturdy friar' to act as look-out. The friar more than played his part; assuming armour under his robe and taking a spear in his hand, he awaited the English on horseback and on their appearance, not content simply to give the alarm, galloped at them himself as Douglas and his men broke from cover. This friar was by no means unusual among Scottish clerics in an enthusiasm for his country's cause too great to forbear arms; a few years earlier the bishop of Dunkeld had led the men of Fife in repelling a sea-borne English raid, and at least one of Douglas's chaplains rode armed into battle behind his lord.

The forage party had been a large one and its losses, said to have been more than three hundred men, sufficed to frighten the English out of further forays. This affair may also unfortunately have contributed to the spleen Edward now vented on the abbeys of Melrose and Kelso, both of which were wholly destroyed by the retreating English.* The burning of buildings and the killing of a few monks too ill or old to escape was about all the English army was now fit for. By the time it recrossed the border, about 1 September, the condition of the soldiery was so poor that there was nothing to do but disband them at once; nor were the losses of this ill-fated campaign even now at an end, for many of the half-starved men, returning to plenty, ate so greedily as to die of surfeit. Despite this failure Edward had not abandoned his intention of settling the Scottish affair for good, and he now decided to winter in the north, for its safety, and re-open hostilities the following year. The choice, however, no longer lay with him. The King of Scots was on the move again.

On 30 September, with an army comprising not only the troops of the Steward, Douglas and Moray but also the Highlanders that he retained under his own control, Robert crossed the Solway and marched into Westmorland. For a few days he lay at Beaumont near Carlisle, while his troops wasted the surrounding country and scouts cast about for news of the English king, then, learning that Edward was in the Cleveland Hills, he plucked his men from their pillaging, crossed the Pennines and marched down into the plain of the Ouse. The Scots were passing Northallerton before Edward, now at Rievaulx† in the south-west corner of the Clevelands, realized his danger. On 13 October he sent out frantic summonses to Pembroke and Harcla to gather troops and join him as quickly as they could. Next morning the Scots, pressing forward with all the speed they might, saw rising before them from the plain the steep and sudden escarpment of the Hambleton Hills.

The approach to Rievaulx was by a narrow path up that escarpment; probably, since the routes of roads in difficult country change little with the centuries, on the line of the modern motor road up Sutton Bank, the gradients of which are even now in places one in four. This path, now held by the troops of John of Brittany, earl of Richmond, formed an eminently defensible position which nevertheless must be stormed if Edward were to

* In March 1326, Robert granted to the monks of Melrose, to rebuild their abbey, the dues of royal justice in Roxburghshire up to the amount of £20,000. Douglas was appointed super-auditor of their collection.
† Not, as Barbour states, at Byland, which nevertheless gave its name to the battle of 14 October.

be captured; the only other way to Rievaulx went roundabout, south of the hills and in by the gap at Helmsley, and long before they could cover it the bird would have flown. In a hasty conference between King Robert and his commanders it was decided that Douglas's battalion should make a frontal assault on the path while Robert with the Highlanders, lightly armed men who excelled other troops in their agility, sought a way to climb the wooded slopes away from the path, to gain the height unseen and take its defenders in flank.* The Steward was commanding the cavalry; attack on so steep a position being impossible to them, their role was to dash through, as soon as the way was cleared, to Rievaulx to capture Edward.

To Moray no part had been assigned, and he could not bear to be left out of so promising a battle. When he saw the Borderers forming up before the hill he went over, attended only by three squires, to join them; and Douglas, coming round to inspect his men before leading them to the attack, was startled to see the earl beaming at him from the front rank. So broad and so friendly a hint could not be ignored, and Douglas invited Moray to join him in leading the assault against the hostile steep.

A vigorous attack carried them some distance up, but there they were held. The English troops, led by Sir Thomas Ughtred and Sir Ralph Cobham, were in a strong position astride a precipitous and wooded road and made good use of it, pouring arrows into the Scots and rolling boulders down the hill against them. The Scots, though in the fury of their assault they put Cobham to flight and captured Ughtred, failed to carry the crest, and for a while the battle swayed to and fro beneath it. Then from above there sounded the clamour of another fight, the English troops recoiled, and Douglas rallied his men in a fresh assault that carried them over the top and on to the plateau beyond, where Robert and his Highlanders were smashing into the English rear. The battle was effectively over. Walter Steward and the cavalry tore past on their way to Rievaulx, and the Scots set about the congenial task of taking prisoners; John of Brittany, himself among the captured,

---

* Barbour says that Robert decided on the flank movement without premeditation when the frontal assault hung fire. But the actual shape of this battle, an overt frontal movement combined with an assault from concealment, so closely resembles that of Pass of Brander and of the capture of Edinburgh as to suggest it was intended from the start.

had to endure a personal tongue-lashing from Robert as well as the knowledge of defeat and the prospect of paying a heavy ransom. Surprisingly, the prisoners were found to include several French knights—three of them, with their squires, the prisoners of Douglas—among them the Seigneur de Sully, French envoy to Edward. Robert was anxious to secure the positive support of the King of France, whose influence with the Pope would be of value to him, and forgave their offence in taking up arms against a sovereign with whom their king was at peace; going farther, he released them without ransom, and with gifts. This generosity was to be wholly without effect on the French king, but Sully himself was grateful and later did what was in his power to help Robert in bringing about an accommodation both with the English and with the Pope.

At Rievaulx Robert moved into Edward's hastily abandoned quarters, still strewn with his personal baggage, his furnishings and his silver plate, not to mention his privy seal, which the Scots now seized for the second time. Edward himself had escaped, scurrying first to Bridlington and then to York in a flight that shocked his people. Though English losses at Byland were far less than those at Bannockburn the humiliation of this defeat, occurring as it did deep in England, was even more keenly felt. 'What greater shame could befall the English', cried the Bridlington chronicler, 'than that their King in his own kingdom be hunted from place to place by the Scots while his people scatter here and there like a flock unshepherded before its enemies?' One Englishman at least was trying to get the shepherd back to the flock. Andrew Harcla went to Edward at York with the troops he had raised in response to the summons of 13 October and begged him to lead them against the Scots, but Edward, 'ever chicken-hearted and luckless in war',* would not agree, and Harcla left in disgust. 'The Scots were so fierce, and their chiefs so daring, and the English so badly cowed, that it was no otherwise between them than as a hare before greyhounds', wrote Gray.

The greyhounds now had at their disposal the Wold as far as Humberside, virgin territory to them, and were making the most of it. Robert pitched his camp at Malton while his troops introduced to this new country the blackmail by fire and plunder long familiar to the north. The Bridlington chronicler gives a lively

* *Lanercost Chronicle.*

picture of one monastery's response to it. As soon as the disaster at Byland was learned of (from Edward in person, this monastery having been his first place of refuge) the portable treasures of the place—chalices, vestments, relics, even the crucifix—were parcelled up and dispatched to the monastery's church at Goxhill, south of the Humber. The monks next took thought for the protection of their estate, and one of their number, who had kinsmen among the Scots, was sent to Malton to negotiate an indemnity. He returned accompanied by nine Scots with eighteen horses, the spares for loading with the meat, bread and wine that were to be the price of Bridlington's immunity. Once they were gone the monks, relieved of material fears, were attacked by spiritual ones. They had been trafficking with excommunicates; what of their souls? But an anxious letter to the archbishop of York brought them absolution and they could be at ease again, at least until the Scots came back. They had got off more lightly than Beverley, which had to pay £400 in tribute, while Ripon was burned to the ground.

The Scots returned home on 1 November. Two months later King Robert, then at Lochmaben, was visited by Andrew Harcla, earl of Carlisle.

Harcla had at last realized that Edward neither could defend his people in war nor would give them safety by peace. He had therefore determined that peace must if necessary be imposed on the king, and had come to the King of Scots in the hope of negotiating terms. Robert was prepared to treat without taking any advantage from this evidence of further disaffection in Edward's realm, and the provisional terms he agreed with Harcla manifested a generosity that should have done much to help Harcla render complaisant to Edward the primary condition that Scottish independence must be recognized. If Edward accepted this within twelve months, Robert undertook not only to found a monastery for the good of the souls of those dead in the war, but to pay the English king £27,000. With this offer Harcla returned to Cumberland to try to build up in the north a party strong enough to enforce on Edward agreement to those proposals.

But Harcla, despairing too late, had himself already sawn off the branch he now wanted to sit on. The northern lords who would have supported such a measure had made their throw a year earlier, and died in the proscriptions that followed Boroughbridge. To their followers and kinsmen who survived them Harcla was the man who, more than any other save the king himself, had been responsible for those deaths. Though the common folk rejoiced at the prospect of an end to the sufferings so long inflicted on them by the Scots, the northern magnates concurred in Harcla's plans unwillingly and 'more from fear than liking' (*Lanercost Chronicle*). Thus when his activities came, as they quickly did, to the ear of Edward, who saw in them plain treason, Harcla was easily arrested by a group of local knights whom he thought he could trust. Tried and found guilty as a traitor, he was condemned to undergo first degradation and then execution. On 3 March his comital belt was ripped off and his gilded spurs were struck from his heels before he underwent the full penalty of hanging, beheading and quartering. Thomas of Lancaster had been spared the sentence in its fullness for his nearness of blood to the king, but no such leniency was shown the man who had done more than any other Englishman living to defend his people against the Scots. On the gallows Harcla declared his innocence of any treasonable intent, insisting that he had been moved to do only what he believed best for the people.

More than any other Englishman of the time, Harcla was Douglas's counterpart. The two men were both Marchers, Harcla by birth and Douglas by adoption, both professional soldiers whose advancement was founded on military achievement, both actuated by awareness of an obligation to the folk below them as well as to the king above. But for Douglas all the currents of his life—talents, interest, affections, fealty to his king and responsibility to his people—set in the same direction; the contrary pulls of fealty and responsibility brought in the end literal dismemberment to the man who served Edward Plantagenet and not Robert Bruce.

Chapter 8

The Truce that Failed

> Let him who desires peace, prepare for war.
> Vegetius

Three months after Harcla's execution, Edward vindicated the dead man's judgment by entering into a thirteen-year truce with Robert. The terms (in the settlement of which Sully acted as intermediary) provided for the reciprocal surrender of occupied territory, for the establishment of a demilitarized zone along the Border, and for the free passage of foreign merchants; they provided, too, that Edward would offer no impediment to Robert's efforts to reconcile himself with the Pope. The armistice did not amount even to a simulacrum of peace—it was expressly laid down that neither English nor Scots should cross the Border without a pass from the appropriate warden—but it was Robert's hope that so prolonged a period of truce would permit the gradual acceptance by the English of Scotland's independent existence, and so open the way to a permanent settlement between the two nations.

For the first time since his childhood Douglas, now in his late thirties, could contemplate a future not dominated by war or the needs of war. For him, however, this cannot have meant settling down to the peacetime life of a country gentleman, even had he any idea what this was like. Whether in peace or war, he was now one of the most important men in Scotland as well as being, thanks to Robert's grants, one of the wealthiest. His estates now far exceeded the patrimony he had taken up arms to regain. Their full total is uncertain, for few of his charters survive and the rolls that list Robert's charters in abstract are damaged and may be incomplete, but at this time they included, besides Douglas itself and the neighbouring parish of Carmichael (which may have been a part of the Douglas heritage), Polbuthy in Moffatdale; the barony of Staplegorton and half that of Westerkirk, in Eskdale; Cockburn; Bedrule in Teviotdale; and Romanno in Peeblesshire. As constable of Lauder he held Lauderdale, and as governor of Jedburgh the town and castle, with Bonjedward. And if, with no warfare or raiding in which to work off his superabundant energy, he wished to hunt, he was lord of the forests of Ettrick, Selkirk, Traquair and Jedburgh, virtually the Forest itself by its official titles, the greatest hunting-ground in southern Scotland.

All the king's grants to Douglas lay on or within reach of the Border, and there can be little doubt that Robert deliberately established his friend as the dominant power in the marches, as he had his nephew in the north and his son-in-law in the central Lowlands. Later kings of Scotland would have cause to deplore this tremendous concentration of power in one family, but Robert had problems enough of his own without worrying about posterity's, and from his point of view it made sense to extend the authority in Scotland's most vulnerable region of his ablest general and closest friend.

James was not the only Douglas to be enriched by royal grants. His rise had naturally ensured the convergence of his kinsmen at his side, and by the end of the reign not only his Lothian cousins but his half-brother Archibald were to be counted among the recipients of Robert's bounty. Archibald and his elder brother Hugh had been brought up in England, where their mother had married for a third time, but for people called Douglas the prospects were obviously brighter in Scotland, and at some unknown date both came north. Hugh, who had taken orders, was provided for with a prebend of Glasgow Cathedral, possibly that of Old Roxburgh, which he certainly held in 1346. Since Hugh was later to succeed his nephew William as lord of Douglas, and his succession was not barred by incapacity, he cannot have been mentally deficient, but he appears to have been singularly inert. His sole recorded action in his clerical capacity is the casting of a vote by proxy at a meeting of the chapter of the diocese of Glasgow in 1325, and as lord of Douglas he seems to have been ruled by his cousin, William Douglas of the Lothian branch. Stupidity was common among Douglases, but torpidity was not, and later generations would remember Hugh as the Dull Douglas.

Archibald, on the other hand, appears to have inherited to the full the misdirected energy that characterized so many of the family. In this youngest son, whose cognomen was to be Tineman, the loser, William le Hardi had squared his genetic account with Scotland. In James Sir William had sired the greatest soldier, bar one, the country bred in the Middle Ages, and in Archibald the man who would lead Scotland to her worst defeat before Flodden. During James's lifetime little is heard of Archibald, who appears to have followed his half-brother's banner and discharged adequately the tasks assigned him. He benefited greatly from Robert's generosity, having bestowed on him Morebattle in Roxburghshire, Kirkandrews in Dumfriesshire, and in Buchan, which Robert was resettling with his adherents, Rattray, Crimond and other once Comyn lands. These grants may, however, have been made as much for his half-brother's sake or for that of his father-in-law, Robert's old friend Alexander Lindsay, as for his own. Archibald's conduct after James's death suggests in a minor key something of the delinquent tendencies his father also manifested when well on in maturity. A neighbour at Faudon charged him with dispossession of rights, while the priory of Coldingham complained that with his nephew William he had unlawfully withheld their town of Swinton, priory property granted to James personally 'to have his counsel and his aid in time of war', and William, a minor, is unlikely to have been the instigator in this dispossession. Possibly Archibald had the wardship of his nephew; if so, it may have been his control of the vast Douglas estates as much as his name that secured him the short and lethal regency* that ended at Halidon Hill. Archibald's closest friend was a kinsman in whom also, even more strongly, the Douglas lawlessness would later emerge—William Douglas of Lothian, afterwards famous and then notorious as 'the dark knight of Liddesdale', who stood godfather to Archibald's second son; the godson was eventually to kill the godfather.

In 1324 the birth of a son to Queen Elizabeth, after twenty-two years of marriage and two daughters, occasioned general rejoicing in Scotland despite the obvious fact that the chance of a royal minority—Robert was now nearly fifty and his health was deteriorating—was greatly increased thereby. The thought of his

---

* During which, it was later said, he used his powers to alienate crown property to his nephew.

death would have moved grief but not alarm in a country secure in the possession of two regents-designate who were among the outstanding soldier-statesmen of the day.

For these two the suspension of war cannot have meant, any more than for Robert, much lessening in their preoccupation with public affairs. Moray almost at once turned or was directed to diplomacy, while Douglas's great estates can seldom have seen more than fleetingly a lord almost constantly in attendance on the king. Douglas probably spent more time with Robert now than during the fighting years, when they had often been continuously engaged on different fronts. He may at least have been able, when the court was in the Lowlands, to enjoy the produce of his nearer estates, if not indeed to visit and to entertain the king on them, and while in Berwick, a town Robert frequently stayed in during the years of truce, may have lived at the property Robert had given him in the Hidegate there. It was at Berwick that he received from the king what was to be the most famous of all the Douglas charters. This, the 'Emerald Charter', was granted ostensibly in consideration of Douglas's surrender to the king of the Frenchmen he had taken prisoner at Byland. These prisoners had of course been, by the understanding of the age, Douglas's property, and in giving them up so that Robert could release them free of ransom he had been parting with something entirely his, the value of which was reckoned at 4,400 marks.* By way of partial compensation, the king now granted to him, in all lands in Scotland he held in chief, full criminal jurisdiction with the profits thereof, excepting only manslaughter and the pleas of the Crown, and freed him and his heirs for ever of all suits of court, wardings of castles and other feudal services excepting only common aid for the defence of the realm. This gift was made in no niggardly fashion; its benefits were explicitly to endure for ever. 'And that this charter to the same James and his heirs may in perpetuity stand firm as an oak we have by way of seisin placed with our own hand on the hand of the said James a ring set with a stone called an emerald.'

It was on 8 November 1324 that the emerald ring passed from one big, sinewy hand to the other. The following February Douglas was again, or still, with the king at Arbroath, where he witnessed a charter of lands to Alexander Keith, and whence he

* £2,933.6s.8d. A mark was two-thirds of a pound.

returned with Robert to Berwick where on the 24th the king made his dear and faithful James of Douglas the further valuable grant of Buittle in Galloway. In March he attended a parliament the king held at Scone, and later that year accompanied old bishop Lamberton on a visit to the king at Tarbert Castle; the constable's account roll, the oldest surviving in Scotland, notes a payment of 2s. 2½d. for birch boughs to strew the floors of their rooms. It was at Tarbert that Robert then kept the great ship he used for cruising among the Western Isles, and Douglas may have joined him on one of these excursions. Almost twenty years had passed since they had first sailed these waters together in very different case, their galleys in flight before their enemies and James at least hauling an unaccustomed oar, and the years between had seen every gain they dreamed of but one: English recognition of Scottish independence.

This seemed as far away as ever. It was now quite plain that Edward had no intention of letting the truce mature into peace, or even of observing its terms. How little he felt himself bound by these had been manifest as early as 1323, when Moray had gone to Avignon as Robert's ambassador to plead for removal of the sentences of interdict and excommunication on the Scots. In breach of his specific undertaking Edward had sent his own envoy (the chronicler Murimuth) to oppose Moray, and, despite Sully's personal advocacy of the Scottish case, to do so successfully. Moray's mission had not, however, been entirely without gain, for he had managed at last to secure papal recognition of Robert's title. Relations with England had not since improved. The frontier control remained rigorous, Edward rebuking the English wardens for issuing too many passes, and when in 1326 English ships seized and English municipal officers imprisoned Scottish merchants travelling in English and in neutral ships, Robert's requests for redress were ignored.

That year Moray again set off on diplomatic business, this time to France to renew the treaty of mutual friendship negotiated in the days of the Guardians. This mission resulted in the treaty of Corbeuil, foundation of the Auld Alliance in which Scotland was always, on the whole, to give more than she got. France had already shown herself an unreliable ally, but common hostility, the normal basis of alliance, offered no alternative to a country whose enemy was England. The belief at least that Scotland was not without friends may have brought the Scots some comfort.

With this treaty Moray was able to bring back from France the latest instalment in the scandalous story that every court in Europe was now enjoying, which must have been peculiarly delicious to the Scots as concerning the English king. Edward never learned. Relieved through no achievement of his own of the domestic enemies he had raised up for himself, he promptly set about making more. When a dispute with France over the Gascon border erupted into violence, he relieved his feelings not merely by arresting all Frenchmen in England but by sequestering the estates and dismissing the attendants of his French queen, on whom he then imposed Hugh Despenser's wife as controller of her household. Isabelle dissembled her resentment so well that when negotiations with France were re-opened her offer to act as her husband's ambassadress was accepted. When she wrote from Paris that the French king insisted on Edward's still unperformed homage for Aquitaine he himself, prompted by Despenser, who feared to let the king out of his control, suggested that their eldest son be vested with the duchy and discharge the obligation in his stead. Isabelle gladly accepted and the heir apparent set sail. It was only when this trump card was safely in his mother's hands that Edward learned that his wife was now the mistress of his greatest enemy outside Scotland, Roger Mortimer of Wigmore, the unsuccessful rebel, who had escaped from the Tower and fled to France two years earlier. A summons to her to return proving fruitless—she dared not, she wrote, go home for fear of Hugh Despenser—the outraged cuckold wrote to the King of France and the Pope demanding that they compel his wife to go back to him. This proved effective in so far as it stimulated King Charles to deny his sister further protection, and with her son and Mortimer she left Paris for Ponthieu, and later Hainault, at about the time of Moray's mission there.

King Robert and Douglas could enjoy this gossip with a clear conscience, for politically a breach between Edward and his wife had significant potential. A few months transformed this into actuality. In September the exiles landed at Harwich, with a force of soldiery supplied by the count of Hainault and led by his brother Jean, to become the rallying-point for all the enemies Hugh Despenser had made for himself and Edward. It is a measure of Edward's failure as ruler that the vast majority of Englishmen looked on indifferently while rebels backed by foreign troops marched against their king; of his failure as a human being, that his every adult relative joined his overthrowers. Retreating westward as Isabelle and Mortimer advanced, he was taken at last in South Wales on 16 November with Despenser, soon to be hanged, drawn and quartered at Hereford. On 7 January 1327, a parliament convoked for the purpose offered the crown to Edward's son. A fortnight later Edward, now a prisoner at Kenilworth, was pressurized into a form of abdication, and the reign of Edward III began.

What ultimately brought Edward of Caernarvon to ruin was less his incompetence than his bad manners. Inferior to his great adversary as ruler and as general, he was no less inferior as a social being. Robert Bruce's charm was admitted even by the English chronicler Trokelowe, who wrote of him that after Bannockburn 'he treated his prisoners so graciously and courteously that the hearts of many who were opposed to him he amazingly turned to feeling affection for him'. While Robert made friends of enemies, Edward, too selfish for kindliness and too stupid to counterfeit it, made enemies of those who should have been his friends. Feckless, partial, unreliable as he was, he might, like his grandfather Henry III whom he resembled in all this and whose mismanagement had been no less than his, have died in his bed still King of England had it not been for the disregard of other people's sensitivities that fuelled with personal resentment the political hostility that brought him at last to deposition, and to his dreadful end at Berkeley Castle eight months later.

Chapter 9

The Perfection of a General's Skill

> I am no advocate of battles, especially at the outset of a war; and I am convinced that an able general can manage, his whole life through, to avoid being brought to battle. Nothing is more depressing to the enemy than this method; nothing more advances one's objectives. . . . My point is that one can wage war without taking risks, and that to do so is the peak and the perfection of a general's skill.
>
> Maurice de Saxe

The events in England in the winter of 1326-7 were naturally watched with the closest attention by Robert and his councillors, anxious to discern whether a change of power in England would mean a change of policy towards Scotland. The decision on their own attitude could not long be deferred. The deposition of Edward technically abrogated the truce he had sealed, and the new government in England—which in practice meant Isabelle and Mortimer—made haste to offer a renewal. This might seem promising, but less encouraging was the knowledge that Edward's loss of Scotland had figured prominently among the grounds for his deposition. Further reason for hesitating to tie their hands anew may have lain in the realization that time now might not be in Scotland's favour. The original truce was to have run till 1336. By then a generation unaccustomed to war would have grown up in Scotland, Robert if he lived would be over sixty and his heir still a child, Moray and Douglas would be about fifty, almost old men by the standards of the day, and England's new king, who might yet prove himself less the son of Edward II than the grandson of Edward I, would be a young man in his prime. When on the night of 1 February—the date of young Edward's coronation at Westminster—a troop of Scots crossed the Tweed for an unsuccessful assault on Norham Castle, their action, though probably unauthorized by the king, reflected the conclusions towards which he was tending.

Envoys were sent to York to treat with the English concerning a renewal of the truce, but what both sides were preparing for as the negotiations dragged on into the spring was a renewal of the war. The English government, which had circulated throughout the kingdom writs for military preparations as early as 5 April, on 16 May issued pardons to a number of criminals on condition they served against the Scots, and soon after a thousand men-at-arms under the earl of Lancaster, younger brother of the late Thomas, the earl of Kent, half-brother of Edward II, and the lords Wake, de Ros, Beaumont and Mowbray, were sent to Newcastle for the protection of the March.

In June the negotiations at York finally broke down, the Scottish envoys took their leave, pausing only to pin a rude rhyme on a church door,* and Douglas crossed the Border to flaunt his banner through the northern counties in a chevauchée which if not specifically intended to restore morale on both sides to its pre-truce condition certainly had that effect. The blue-blooded warriors from Newcastle had no difficulty in locating a force whose progress was punctuated by pillars of smoke; halting it was another matter. 'James of Douglas went before them at a distance of four leagues, burning and wasting the land in open sight of them all; for none of them dared go forth, so grievously were they demoralised and unprepared for war.'† This little excursion was no more than an *hors d'œuvre* for Douglas, who returned from it only to depart soon after with Moray for the far more important operation that represented for the Scots the opening of a new strategy.

Although since the recapture of Berwick fighting had been almost exclusively on English soil, war in the enemy's country had

---

* 'Long beards heartless, painted hoods witless, gay cloaks graceless, make England thriftless', according to the *Brut* chronicle.
† *Scalacronica*, translated by Sir Herbert Maxwell.

been for Robert part of an essentially defensive strategy. The Scots had been sincere in their claim to be fighting a war forced on them and maintained solely to secure their country's independence; there had been nothing expansionist about their aims. In its primary object this policy had failed, for Scottish independence was no nearer to being recognized than before. The weakness of the Scottish policy had all along been that it gave the English—other than the battered and unheeded northerners—no incentive to end the war. Success would bring them Scotland and failure would lose them nothing of England. In 1327, however, the Scots evidently decided to try the gambit—suggested perhaps by Douglas or Moray rather than by the ailing king—of acting as if with the intention of annexing English territory. To be credible, however, a threat of this kind must be preceded by a reminder of Scottish ability to implement it. This necessary demonstration was now the objective of Douglas and Moray.

Robert had crossed to Ireland, there to intimidate the English seneschal of Ulster into granting him a truce for a year together with food supplies, and was still absent when early in July his generals crossed the border. The force they headed was a substantial one, including beside their own following not only the Steward's—led by James Stewart since the death of his elder brother Walter the previous year—but also that of the earl of Mar.* This host, though far from representing the full military resources of Scotland, was no raiding party but an army prepared and intending to try conclusions with the national force known to be mustering in England, and, since Donald of Mar, joint commander with Douglas and Moray by virtue of rank, had at least sense enough to do what he was told, and Moray would always in the last resort yield to his colleague, its effective commander-in-chief was Douglas.

The prospect before him was stimulating. The English, filled with the euphoria of a new reign, were as ready as the Scots for a fresh encounter, and preparing far more lavishly against it. Forty-three towns had been ordered to send levies—London alone

---

* Donald of Mar, Robert's nephew, captured as a child by the English in 1306 and brought up in the household of Edward II, had after Bannockburn chosen to remain in England, till on his patron's downfall he had fled to Robert in the hope of raising Scottish aid towards Edward's restoration, and had been regranted his earldom.

responding with 70 men-at-arms, 30 hobelars, and 164 foot archers—while supply fleets had been ordered to concentrate at Skinburness and at Yarmouth. The government, moreover, not content with domestic resources, had hired Jean of Hainault, their ally of the previous year, to bring a troop of auxiliaries to their support, and just before Easter he had arrived in York with more than five hundred men-at-arms in his train, among them a Liégeois by the name of Jean Le Bel, who thirty years later recorded in his chronicle of his own times his recollections of the campaign that followed.*

The army was nominally to be led by the fifteen-year-old king, already dreaming of military glory; in practice its command appears to have been divided, not to say disputed, among Henry, earl of Lancaster, the Earl Marshal (Thomas of Brotherton, Edward's young half-uncle), and Jean of Hainault. Mortimer, reflecting perhaps that in the previous reign few English magnates had confronted the Scots without loss of credit, abstained from participation.

The hosting at York, gay with festivities in honour of Jean of Hainault, was unpleasantly marred when a quarrel at dice led to fighting between the English archers and the Hainaulters, and a number of deaths. A hastily convened enquiry assigned blame to the Englishmen, which did nothing to sweeten the tempers of the archers, and relations grew so bad that the Hainaulters dared not venture into the city save armed and in large numbers. It was felt that, the military initiative having as so often in the previous reign been left to the Scots, the sooner they exercised it and provided a more suitable focus for hostility the better. There was thus general relief when Edward, having received word that Scots raiders had been seen in Westmorland on 4 July, ordered a move to join the advanced troops in Durham. There it was, a few days later, that he learned that the Scots were actually near at hand, having moved so unobtrusively that it was the smoke of villages burning near Durham that first told the English their whereabouts. On 17 July young Edward rode out at the head of his first army to pursue and punish the Scots, blissfully unaware that he was embarking on one of the most farcical episodes in the history of war.

Pursuit was what Douglas wanted. He fully intended to face

* It was on this chronicle that Froissart based his account of the 1327 campaign, and of the deaths of Bruce and Douglas.

the English in due course, in his own time and on his own ground, and meanwhile a chase could do nothing but harm the morale of the English. They could not overtake him till he chose, and until then he could lead them a terrible dance. The Scots had by now perfected the technique of fast and unencumbered movement on campaign. Their commissariat the oats in their saddlebags and the lifted cattle driven before them, their armament on their backs, their modest camping equipment trussed on packhorses, they could travel at a speed far exceeding their pursuers' and their road was any ground over which hooves could go. Away went the fox south-westward up Wear and thence, probably by the Gaunless valley, over into Teesdale; and five leagues after, recounts Le Bel, 'through woods and swamps and wildernesses, and evil mountains and valleys', lumbered the English and their auxiliaries, their sutlers and their baggage-waggons, their wine-barrels, sides of meat and loads of fodder, camp-kitchens and baled-up pavilions and all the paraphernalia essential to well-bred Englishmen and Hainaulters on active service. From Teesdale Douglas swung north into the moors and over toward the Wear again, apparently so confident the English must dance to his tune that for once he did not trouble to keep in touch with their movements by scouting. There was, after all, no risk that they might lose their way, for the Scots in their usual fashion were literally blazing a trail through the country. On 19 or 20 July the Scots bivouacked among the hills south of the Wear, near Stanhope. Not far off, Douglas, reconnoitring the country, found the site on which if anywhere he would be ready to give battle. The first camp was broken, the Scots moved to the new position, pitched camp again, and waited for the coming of the enemy; and continued to wait. The English army had vanished.

On the morrow rain began to fall, settling into a steady downpour that soaked the ground and swelled the river and drenched men and beasts and firewood. The Scots stayed where they were. More than rain was needed to dismay men inured to campaigning in harsher weather than July could furnish, and the English army, wherever it might be, would be getting just as wet. They were in England, they had looted and burned to their hearts' content and they had with them plenty of oatmeal and English cattle in ample numbers to supply their customary dull but adequate camp diet of porridge and boiled beef. Douglas himself saw no reason to abandon a satisfactory position. The English, who wanted to fight him more than he did them, would find it sooner or later, and the army was provisioned for a fortnight or more. He could wait. He dispatched a troop under his brother Archibald to raid the bishopric of Durham, and set about acquainting himself with his chosen terrain till he was fully master of its military potential.

For eight days they waited and it rained, and on the ninth Scottish scouts brought in a captured English squire, one Thomas of Rokesby. Led before Douglas and Moray for questioning, Thomas proved perfectly willing to tell them where the English were, and why. The English commanders, realizing their own inability to overtake the Scots, had sought some other means of forcing battle. The northward swing of the Scots from Teesdale and the breaking up of their first camp near Stanhope had given rise to the belief that they were heading back to Scotland, and this in turn to the inspiration of intercepting and engaging them at the Tyne crossing. A forced march north had carried the English and Hainaulters to Haydon Bridge, where ever since they had awaited, with diminishing expectation, the Scots homeward bound, till at last young Edward, announcing that whoever could bring him within sight of the Scots would be rewarded with a knighthood and land worth £100 a year, had set a score of squires galloping about the hills of Northumberland and Durham. Thomas had chosen the right direction; if only he had seen the Scottish scouts before they saw him he would by now be racing northward to become Sir Thomas with £100 a year.

Forthcoming as Thomas was, he is unlikely to have disclosed to the Scottish commanders the real state of affairs at Haydon Bridge. Le Bel is eloquent on the subject. That forced march from the Wear to the Tyne, an exhausting ride over dreadful country, had entailed leaving behind the entire service corps. The night of arrival at Haydon Bridge—without food other than a loaf of bread per man, tied to saddles and soaked in horse-sweat during the ride, without wine, without fodder, without tents—had been spent under arms beside saddled horses. The next day there had been no food at all. Lacking the Scots techniques of self-sufficiency on campaign, the English and the Hainaulters could only fast till a message from Edward brought traders out from Newcastle with bread and wine to sell at exorbitant prices to the sodden and

THE PERFECTION OF A GENERAL'S SKILL

hungry troops. All the while rain bucketed down on their shelterless heads, swelling the Tyne till the Scots if they came could not ford it, and there was nothing to do but try vainly to stop their horses' backs from galling under wet saddles, and huddle shivering round feeble fires of green wood, and brood over their woes. The Hainaulters had never dreamed war could mean such wretchedness; they yearned to fight the Scots as the one way out of their miserable plight.

Both parties desiring a confrontation and Douglas preferring it at his chosen site, it only remained to get the English there. Since using young Thomas as messenger meant for him the reward that nobody grudged him, he was turned loose with instructions to hurry to Edward and tell him where he could find the Scots. He was also told to say that they were as eager to fight him as he to fight them, a message possibly contributed by Moray; Douglas liked to keep his options open.

The rain stopped, the sun came out, and everybody brightened at the prospect of action. Two days after Thomas's capture, the English vanguard was seen crossing Blanchland Moor north of Weardale, and Douglas, who still liked to reconnoitre for himself, rode out to weigh up the odds against him. The English and their auxiliaries were advancing with banners displayed, in seven columns, in good order, and in numbers so formidable that he must, returning to marshal the Scots into battle order, have congratulated himself on his choice of position.* A little forward of the Scottish camp, it occupied a hillside from which the ground fell away to the south bank of the Wear. Two rocky spurs thrust out from the steep slope and on these two of the three Scots divisions were posted, the third a little withdrawn behind them, and all three beyond bowshot of the river's north bank. The swollen Wear, racing down its boulder-strewn bed, was their first line of defence, and beyond it was the rocky slope that must be stormed by any army that managed to force the river crossing. The defensibility of the position plainly struck the English at once

---

* The numbers reported for this campaign are, as usual, impossibly inflated. Barbour records 10,000 Scots to 'near 50,000' English, Le Bel 23,000 Scots (3,000 knights and squires and 20,000 hobelars) to 61,000 English (7,000 knights and squires, 30,000 foot-soldiers, 24,000 archers) 'not counting camp-followers'. It seems at any rate that the Scots were facing more than twice their own number of combatants.

as, descending about mid-day from the hill north of the Wear, and defiling beyond the river bank, they halted to study the strength from which the Scots confidently regarded them.

A long pause ensued. The English troops dismounted and deployed in battle order a little way back from the river. Pre-battle ceremonies could be observed; knighthoods were conferred, the boy king was paraded before his army. Then it advanced towards the river. The Scots remained halted and there was another long pause. Then Douglas saw a line of archers, escorted by men-at-arms, filing out from the English rear, guessed they were being dispatched to cross the river farther off and break up the Scots from the flank, and adjusted his dispositions to handle a threat which to him was the most dangerous his enemy could employ.

Long before his countrymen grasped that 'every English archer beareth under his girdle twenty-four Scottish lives'* Douglas had realized it, and responded with a measure which led the longbowmen to regard him with a peculiar and justified dread. Every English archer his men could catch suffered the loss of either a right hand or a right eye. This practice derived from hard realism. Prisoners of war were in those days held captive only where there was prospect of ransom; the age saw nothing amiss in killing the unprofitable, who, however, were generally turned loose. But freeing longbowmen unharmed to fight again must to Douglas have meant risking more Scottish lives than English ones were spared, and a mutilation which permitted their release while precluding subsequent use of the bow may have represented his idea of a compromise between the claims of mercy and his people's need. It had, however, a side-effect on which he may also have reckoned. The longbowmen now felt a terror of him that greatly lessened their usefulness in any operations against him; those in Weardale had had to be filled up with wine before being dispatched against his troops.

He was ready for them. Conversant enough by now with the terrain to reckon their probable course, he pulled out the Scottish cavalry under Donald of Mar and his brother Archibald, led them to a covert near the expected line of the English approach and placed them in it with instructions to attack only when he gave the signal. He himself, throwing on a cloak to cover his too famous blazon, rode on towards the archers and, once he was sure they

* Alleged Scottish proverb quoted by Roger Ascham in *Toxophilus*.

had marked him, turned to move with seeming aimlessness in the direction of his ambush. The bait was taken. The half-drunk archers, seeing what looked like a rich prize isolated far out on the Scottish flank, ran excitedly, loosing ineffective arrows, in pursuit. Douglas had them almost where he wanted them when, despite his precaution, he was recognized by an English squire who, galloping madly down the line of archers, shouted that that was Douglas, *Douglas*, and some trick was meant. The name alone would have routed the archers; their panic instantaneous, they were already turning to run when Douglas's summons brought the Scottish cavalry from the wood to ride them down. First blood had gone to the Scots.

Douglas returned to the main Scottish army, still watching from its hillside the English deliberating on the farther bank. After a while heralds detached themselves, crossed the river and rode up to bring from young King Edward a message conceived in the best traditions of chivalry. He proposed that the English should withdraw from the river edge, allowing the Scots to cross unopposed today or to-morrow as pleased them and take up position on the northern side, so that the two armies could fight it out in plain battle; alternatively, let the Scots give the like grace to the English and the battle be fought on the southern bank. Moray and Douglas withdrew to consider the proposal.

Edward's sporting offer—that the Scots fight a larger and better equipped army on level terms as to ground—was received by Douglas in his usual unsporting spirit. On this issue, however, he and Moray were not as one. Moray, who had never quite outgrown the young man who thought his uncle's guerrilla tactics unchivalrous, became very martial, swearing that he would fight however great the opposing odds. Douglas however, careful as always of Scottish lives, had no intention of risking them on adverse terms, and he applied all his powers of cajolery ('God be praised that we have so valiant a captain') and argument ('there is no discredit to the weaker side in using what advantage it can gain') to bring his colleague to his way of thought.* He

* Barbour places this discussion immediately after Douglas's return from reconnaissance. Moray, however, could not then have foreseen that the English would not attack across the river—Douglas was ready to fight had they done so—and it seems likelier to have been Edward's message, which Barbour does not mention, that touched off his inconvenient fit of gentlemanliness.

succeeded, even inducing Moray to concur in returning the heralds an answer which was not in the best traditions of chivalry at all (Le Bel).

> They said they would do neither the one nor the other. They said that, as the king and his staff could see, they were in his realm and had burned it and wasted it; and if this vexed him he could come and stop them, for they would stay where they were for as long as they pleased.

The heralds returned, and after a while the marshalled ranks beyond the river were seen breaking up to pitch camp. The English, too, were staying where they were.

The Scots broke position to make ready for night, curiously studying the opposite camp and observing there two novelties they had not seen before. One was the wearing of heraldic devices as helmet-crests; the Scots thought they were lovely. The other was cannon. These seem to have been unused throughout the campaign, the preceding week's rain having perhaps spoilt the gunpowder, and even had they been employed would probably—so inaccurate were these primitive engines, that endangered their users scarcely less than their targets—have done the Scots little harm. Even Douglas, alert though he was to the implications of projectile weapons, can hardly have recognized in the strange, vase-shaped objects the English dragged about with them a death-warrant for the system of personal warfare that had been the theatre of his own achievement.

Night fell and the armies settled, but not to sleep. The Scottish soldiery had by now grasped Douglas's idea that unnerving the enemy was a useful activity, and they set about it with a will. Building up enormous fires, they sat round them all night, alternately blasting on their horns and emitting concerted yells 'until it seemed the biggest devils in hell were there to destroy us'. Its effect on Le Bel leaves little room for doubt that the Scottish sacrifice of sleep—the din, keeping awake the enemy a quarter of a mile distant, must in their own camp have been indescribable—reaped its reward.

Next morning both armies resumed their positions of the day before. The English had, it seemed, at last resolved to try and force the river crossing. Their troops being marshalled in battle order, the trumpets sounded and the whole front advanced to the

THE PERFECTION OF A GENERAL'S SKILL

water's edge with a movement so resolute that Douglas and Moray launched the Scots infantry down their hillside to arrest it. Even as they did so one of the pickets Douglas had posted at the rear of the Scottish position rushed up to announce that a large enemy detachment had moved round to the south and was now stationed in a valley behind the Scots. Guessing at once that the seeming assault was a feint to draw the Scots from their strength and expose them to attack from the rear, Douglas raced across the moving front, halted it and returned the infantry to their original places. As they took up station once more the English checked, and in their turn withdrew to their former line. Once more, immobile, the two armies glared at each other across the Wear.

Thus they remained all day, only the young cavalrymen of both sides drawing weapons, as, out on the flanks, 'those who wished to skirmish, skirmished' (Le Bel). These little flurries made no difference to the balance of strength:

> They that ta'en were on a day,
> On another changed were they,

changed, that is, for prisoners taken by their own side. This activity may have been welcome to Douglas as providing an outlet for bellicosities which in his own camp might otherwise have built up into a demand for battle. It would by now have become plain to him that the English were not going to give him the pleasure of defeating them in fight,* and he had probably already determined on a plan—perhaps envisaged as an alternative from the start—for humiliating them by other means. But a strategy long misunderstood even by Moray must have been wholly incomprehensible to an army largely made up of young men who remembered nothing of the disasters that had opened the reign. He had, moreover, to contend with the dangerous euphoria that was one legacy of Bannockburn. Other than Robert himself, Douglas was probably the only Scottish commander to grasp how much they owed that victory to English mismanagement; in nearly all his countrymen Bannockburn had instilled a belief in Scottish invincibility that would cost Scotland many defeats (two of them under commanders, Donald of Mar and Archibald

---

* The *Brut* chronicle records that Henry of Lancaster and Jean of Hainault had wished to attack across the river, but that Thomas of Brotherton opposed them and prevailed.

Douglas, now present in Weardale) before Flodden at last eradicated it. If skirmishing could content these martial spirits, skirmishing was all to the good.

From his actions, it appears that Douglas now founded his strategy on the recognition that battle was a necessary object to the English but not to the Scots. For the Scots, who had succeeded in their ostensible purpose of raiding and looting far into England, unpunished return to Scotland would constitute victory enough. The English stake on victory in battle, however, always large, was now enormous. Their army, representing a financial investment that could not quickly be repeated, had been mustered for two months and nominally in action for a fortnight, and had done nothing but witness the despoliation of the country it was supposed to be defending. Their only hope of recovery, both of money and of face, lay in inflicting a total military defeat upon the Scots.

Since, however, they apparently did not intend to seek it by attacking the ground Douglas had chosen to defend, there was no point in remaining there longer when two miles up the river lay the bishop of Durham's Stanhope hunting-ground. Hilly, wooded and walled, the river before it and a great morass behind, Stanhope Park offered an unassailable position for the Scots to wait out the length of time Douglas deemed necessary to impress on the English their inability to harm him. Orders were given and that night* the Scots quietly struck camp and moved to the Park, leaving their camp fires blazing behind them. By the next morning they were comfortably settled in and ready for the English, whose puzzled scouts appeared about mid-day, to be followed an hour or two later by the entire army squelching grimly upstream to pitch their fresh camp on the opposite bank and sit down again to starve the Scots out.

Douglas had no intention of letting them indulge their hopes in peace. Study of the English dispositions had satisfied him that their standards of picketing fell far short of his own, and he determined to exploit this slackness. Taking with him five hundred carefully briefed men, he rode out after nightfall along the river, forded it well away from either camp and struck into the moorland to circle the English camp and approach it from the rear. As they drew near, Knighton relates, they were seen by some Englishmen, but Douglas, realizing this, at once shouted 'in an English

* Barbour; two nights later, according to Le Bel.

accent, "No ward [watch], by St. George," ' and they, thinking him one of their own captains, let the troop pass unquestioned. The enemy camp lay spread before them, the dark field lit by camp fires round which the common soldiers lay sleeping or chatting, and interspersed with the great muddy mushrooms that were the pavilions of the gentry. Far beyond, splashing the blackness against their horizon, gleamed the fires by which their countrymen crowded to stare across the river and wait the event. With his men Douglas moved quietly on till he was so close he could hear the Englishmen talking round their fires. Then he went in at the gallop.

The Scots knew just what they must do. Half carried spears with which they stabbed down at the men stretched out by their fires, the others swords with which to slash the tent-cords that held the pavilions in place. In a moment the sleepy camp was frantic with cries of alarm, shouts of 'Douglas!' and the cut-off shrieks of men half-wakening to die, while sudden flares from fires kicked apart lit the lurching walls of tents subsiding on to the drowsy and bewildered men within. Le Bel tells how Douglas himself kept on 'most valiantly into the English host, shouting "Douglas! Douglas! You shall all die, lords of England!", killing with his company more than three hundred men, and spurred right on, still yelling "Douglas! Douglas!", as far as the king's tent, and slashed two or three of its cords.' A few moments more and he might have had the big prize kicking across his saddle, but those few could have been too many for his little troop in the great camp where already men were hurrying out in hastily donned armour with weapons in their hands, and Douglas was no gambler. He swung away and sounded his horn in the given signal. Scottish discipline had improved since the capture of Berwick, and the five hundred at once obeyed his call, leaving their prey with a promptitude that got them clear almost without loss, one of the few Scots killed in the whole affair being Douglas's chaplain. But their losses almost included Douglas himself.

He was the last to go, having paused at the edge of the camp to see his people safely clear. It was this solicitude that nearly killed him, for one of the English soldiers, gallantly determined to try and avenge his companions, had stationed himself with a club on the Scottish line of retreat, and when Douglas at last turned away it was to receive his blow. It failed to knock him from his horse; there was a savage little struggle in the darkness, and Douglas rode on. His men, meanwhile, gathering at the ford, had made the alarming discovery of his absence.

> Then were they dreading for him sair;
> Ilkane at other speired tiding,
> But yet of him they heard nae thing.

Hastily they conferred, and resolved to return and seek him, when

> As they were in sic affray,
> A tootling of his horn heard they,

and a moment later he rode down among them. Crowding around him to hear about 'the carle with the club', they forded the river and returned to Stanhope Park, where the rest of the army was waiting under arms. Moray asked eagerly how they had fared, to receive the laconic reply: 'We have drawn blood'. Harking back, perhaps, to a previous disagreement, Moray observed that if all the Scots had joined in the expedition they might have destroyed the English utterly. They might, agreed Douglas imperturbably, and on the other hand they might have been utterly destroyed themselves; he had taken exactly as much risk as he thought justifiable.

Next day the English commanders belatedly gave instructions for pickets to be set out on all sides. These bore harshly on the Hainaulters. They already had to guard themselves against the English archers, who still regarded them with murderous rancour, and now a double watch must be mounted. Sleep became almost impossible, and if they did drop off it was to be wakened by yells of 'The Scots are here!', to stumble into armour, and out to learn of a false alarm. Life by the Wear was proving scarcely more tolerable than by the Tyne. They no longer had the rain, but instead they had the Scots (Le Bel); 'day and night they lived in the greatest fear, dreading the archers and dreading the Scots'. Save for not dreading their archers, the English were in no better case. All were hungry, for even yet the supply waggons had not reached them and they depended still on the provisions traders brought to sell at extortionate prices which they dared not haggle over for fear of reduction to total famine, while their fodderless, almost pastureless destriers were declining before their eyes into saddle-galled skeletons. Hungry, stiff, short of sleep and much shorter of temper, the miserable warriors were buoyed up in spirit by one thought only: all this must end in the annihilation of the Scots. Stanhope Park was now invested on all sides but that closed in by the bog. The Scottish position might be unassailable, but one day soon, when their supplies ran out, the Scots must leave it, try to break the cordon and be totally destroyed.

Moray, too, was convinced the Scots must fight, and as the English lines closed in around the Park he re-opened the issue with his colleague. Would Douglas agree to fight now?

–No, by St Bride.

–Then what *would* Douglas do?

–Douglas would tell him a story.

There was once, he said, a fisherman who had beside the river where he set his nets a little hut in which he used to sleep. One night, when he had been a long while out with his nets, he returned to the hut and found by his fire a fox, eating a salmon he had left there. The fisherman stood in the door and whipped out a sword to kill the fox, who hastily looked around but saw no way out save the door where the fisherman stood. But he saw too the man's cloak lying on the bed, seized it with his teeth and pulled it along till it fell into the fire. The fisherman jumped forward to save his cloak, and the fox streaked past to run in safety to his den, leaving the man to mourn his burnt cloak and his spoiled salmon and his having been tricked by the fox.

We are the fox, said Douglas, and they the fisher. The English thought the Scots had no way out but through their lines; but they were wrong. He had found another path, and if Moray didn't mind getting his feet wet the Scots could trick the English into expecting battle and get clear away without losing as much as one page. He expounded his plan and Moray, content at last, endorsed it.

The next morning, 6 August, preparation began. In the concealment of the wood harness and gear were packed up. Some of the Scots busied themselves cutting branches and binding them into faggots, or gathering firewood, while others shaped the hides of the cattle they had eaten into rough brogues to replace their worn-out shoes. On the other side of the river, in the course of the usual skirmishing, a Scottish knight was 'captured', and on being questioned by the English commanders told them, 'very reluctantly', that orders had been given that that night all the Scots were to arm themselves and follow the banner of Douglas, but nobody knew where. The strung-up English knew what that meant; the Scots were about to attempt a break through their cordon. The cloak was over the fire. That evening the whole English army stood to arms with banners displayed, for the great battle that was going to start at last. The Scots meanwhile were cutting the throats of the remaining cattle and stoking up fiercer bonfires than ever. When night had fallen the removal began. Leaving their camp empty but for two trumpeters blowing their lungs out in an effort to reproduce some semblance of the normal nightly din, the Scots followed Douglas to the edge of the great bog that the English believed impassable and which he long had known was not. The faggots were brought and thrown down on the treacherous ground, and one by one, leading their horses, the Scots began to advance into the quagmire. As the improvised causeway was crossed the faggots were taken up from the rear, passed forward to the front and laid down again on the next stretch of bog, and so on till yard by yard the impassable morass was passed, and without loss

> But if it were a sumpter horse
> That in the moss was left lyand

they were out, muddy and exultant, on the other side.

By daybreak they were bouncing gaily northward, but had not gone far when the foremost scouts saw with surprise the vanguard of another army approaching. Shouting their battle-cry they made ready to fight, only to hear their shouts answered by familiar voices. The approaching host was Scottish, sent out by Robert who, returned from Ireland and worried by the long silence of the army in England, had dispatched this relieving force under the earls of March and Angus.* The Weardale returners gleefully explained that they were in no need of relief, but after three weeks on beef and oatmeal they were glad enough to feast on the provi-

---

* March had turned to the national side in 1315. The Umfraville earls of Angus, who were English, had adhered to Edward and been forfeited; Robert had recently conferred the earldom on John Stewart, the son of Alexander of Bonkle.

sions brought by the earls' troops before the whole force, combining, set off for Scotland in the highest possible spirits.

Douglas's handling of the Weardale affair, the only campaign in which he acted as effectual commander of a major army, is indicative both of his limitations and of his skill in operating within them. He was perhaps the most thoroughly professional soldier of his time, but circumstances had made of him a guerrilla and not a field commander. Formed in the days when Scotland was weak, demoralized and occupied, he had early mastered the techniques of economy in men and materials; his forte had always been the small-scale operation based on good intelligence and designed to weaken the enemy by fear as much as by bloodshed. Except with his own safety, he was no risk-taker. Robert Bruce, a fine field commander and a man capable of venturing much to gain much, might in Weardale have organized, risked and won an open battle; Douglas on the failure of his one attempt to contrive battle on favourable ground eschewed any other, and fell back on the methods in which he had long been adept of baffling, frightening and in the end fooling his enemy. These, however, sufficed, and it is questionable whether any other general of his time could have achieved at so little cost in Scottish blood so great a fiasco for the English as Douglas did in Weardale.

He had left them standing to arms in imminent expectation of Scottish attack, and thus they remained until morning, when the two Scottish trumpeters walked into their camp, gave themselves up and asked what the English were waiting for, with the Scots four or five miles off on their way home. At first the English simply did not believe them, but reconnaissance of the abandoned camp south of Wear soon proved their veracity. The Scots had really gone, and Edward burst into tears. The whole costly expedition, the hiring of the Hainaulters, the ruin of the horses—of which hardly one remained sound—the weeks of discomfort and alarm had gone for nothing but to prove that the Scots could do as they liked in northern England and get away with it. With battle unfought, the English were experiencing the sensations of defeat as fully as the Scots were those of victory. A would-be face-saving announcement was at once concocted, in the form of a writ of summons to parliament declaring that the Scots had fled rather than face the king's army in battle, but nobody was deceived and it was not long before the English were taking refuge in that time-honoured excuse for military failure: 'We were betrayed!'

English impotence duly demonstrated, the Scots moved on to the second phase of their programme. As soon as the Weardale army had rested and refitted, King Robert advanced into Northumberland to begin the motions of annexation to Scotland. Since the few fortresses remaining there were alone, with Newcastle, capable of resistance if not of interference, two of them were at once invested, Robert assigning his own troops to Norham while Douglas and Moray were dispatched to besiege Henry Percy, the English Warden of the Marches, at Alnwick. Robert himself before joining his men at Norham progressed through the county as if it were his own, hunting from park to park and making grants of Northumbrian estates to followers whom, with a nice touch of verisimilitude, he required to pay the sealing fee, the stamp duty of the time. The English Parliament that gathered at Lincoln on 15 September in response to the writs issued from Weardale had more to disquiet it than the August fiasco.

Douglas and Moray must still have been feeling the exhilaration of that jaunt, for they appear to have conducted themselves very frivolously at Alnwick, spending their time in holding jousts until Robert, whose attacks on Norham had evoked an unexpected pugnacious defence from the constable, Sir Robert Manners, summoned them away to join him. Percy, thus relieved, judged the moment opportune for a retaliatory raid into Scotland and set off for Teviotdale with the men of his command as Warden (*Scalacronica*).

> No sooner was James of Douglas informed of this than he suddenly threw himself from Norham with his troops between the said Lord Percy and his castle of Alnwick, which forced Percy to make a night march towards Newcastle, so demoralised were the English in time of war.

That time was almost ended. In the first week of October William Denholm entered the camp at Norham as emissary of the English council, commissioned to treat for peace on the basis of Scottish independence.

Chapter 10

The Reign Fulfilled

> Sleep after toil, port after stormy seas,
> Ease after war, death after life. . . .
>
> Spenser

Towards the end of January 1328, Douglas rode south into England once more. This time his purpose was peace, the hundred Scottish knights who attended him forming merely the ceremonial escort for whose courteous reception in York, where Parliament was meeting, commands had been issued in the name of Edward III. Of himself the resentful young king would never have endorsed the conference that was about to open, but he was still in tutelage to his mother and Mortimer (and also perhaps somewhat distracted with the still younger bride he had just married), and it was with them Douglas had to deal. His mission was to negotiate, on the basis provisionally agreed in correspondence, and to receive parliamentary endorsement of, the terms on which any final treating for peace must be founded. Fundamental was the absolute recognition of Scottish independence, but with this five further points were associated: a marriage between Prince David and an English princess; no restoration of lands forfeited in either country by adherents of the other; an alliance for mutual support against all parties, the French excepted; payment of an indemnity of £20,000 by the Scots; and English aid in securing removal of the excommunication of the Scots.

The negotiations lasted a month, and may not in all respects have proceeded smoothly, the dispatch of five Scots homeward on 15 February in connection with the discussions suggesting that Douglas had found it necessary to refer to Robert for further instructions, or for the endorsement of some concession. The issue in dispute was probably the forfeiture clause, one of the only two not provisionally agreed in principle before Douglas rode south, and the only one not to appear in the final treaty. The 'disinherited' in England, adherents of the English crown who had owned or inherited claims to land in Scotland, were vehemently opposed to giving up their entitlements and included among them men of influence at the English court.* Douglas himself may have found it difficult to press this clause with any great personal ardour; he had not forgotten Faudon. The matter was evidently shelved. Two weeks later letters patent were issued in Edward's name, declaring that:

> Whereas we and some of our predecessors, Kings of England, have attempted to gain rights of rule, superiority or lordship over the Kingdom of Scotland, and terrible hardships have long afflicted the realms of England and Scotland through the wars fought on this account, and bearing in mind the bloodshed, slaughter, atrocities, destruction of churches and innumerable evils from which the inhabitants of both realms have suffered over and over again because of these wars ... we will and concede for us and all our heirs and successors, by the common counsel, assent and consent of the prelates, magnates, earls and barons and communities of our realm in our Parliament, that the Kingdom of Scotland shall remain for ever separate from the Kingdom of England, in its entirety, free and in peace, without any kind of subjection, servitude, claim or demand, with its rightful boundaries as they were held and preserved in the time of Alexander of good memory, King of Scots last deceased, to the magnificent prince the lord Robert, by God's grace illustrious King of Scots, our ally and very good friend, and to his heirs and successors.

The great hurdle had been leaped, and Douglas could return to Scotland—whither the negotiations were now adjourned for the final hammering out of the details of the treaty—bearing with him the vindication of Wallace and Andrew Murray, of Wishart, Atholl and Simon Fraser, of his own father and of all the un-

* Their determination to overset their forfeiture was to lead to the resumption of the Anglo-Scottish war in 1332.

numbered Scottish dead in that long war. It was the first day of March, the month in which, twenty-two years before, he had attended the precarious coronation of Robert Bruce; in which, thirty-two years before, his father had watched from Berwick Castle the army of Edward I approaching to open the war; in which, all his lifetime before, Alexander III had died and Scotland's long crisis begun.

The pill had been a bitter one for the English to swallow, and Isabelle and Mortimer, having forced it down, seem to have been as anxious as the Scots to press the matter to a swift conclusion. The English plenipotentiaries were in Edinburgh by 10 March, and within a week the terms of the treaty had been approved by the Scottish Parliament. On 17 March King Robert sealed them in his chamber in the monastery of Holyrood. In return for England's acknowledgment of Scottish independence and promise of support in seeking the removal of the papal excommunication, they bound Scotland to pay the indemnity of £20,000 (destined, most of it, for the pockets of Queen Isabelle and Mortimer); betrothed Prince David to Joan of the Tower, Edward III's younger sister; and pledged Scotland to alliance with England save against France. First witness to the sealing was the bishop of St Andrews, William Lamberton, an old man within a few months of death who had survived just long enough to see a lifetime's hopes fulfilled, followed by the bishops of Glasgow, Dunkeld, Moray, Dunblane, Ross and Galloway, the earls of Moray, Fife, March, Menteith, Ross and Mar, Sir Robert Lauder, justiciar of Lothian, and James, lord of Douglas. On 4 May the treaty was finally ratified by the English Parliament at Northampton and the War of Independence was at an end.

The royal household at once set about preparing for the occasion that should symbolize the amity of the late belligerents, the wedding of Prince David and Princess Joan, appointed at Berwick in July. These preparations, some record of which survives in the Exchequer Rolls of Scotland, were of the most lavish order. A single commission to one Flemish merchant covered, besides the purchase of cloth and furs to make liveries for the knights and squires of the household, that of 4,360 lb. of almonds, 600 lb. of rice, 378 loaves of sugar, 180 lb. of pepper and 55 lb. of mace, besides nutmegs, cloves, galingale and other assorted spices, 200 st. of wax and 20 tuns of wine. Another account records the purchase of a gold seal and silver-gilt chain for the king's wear at the wedding, but when it came about he was absent. The reason given was illness, and his health certainly had long been poor—the previous year, in Ireland, he had been thought dying—but on this occasion he may have suffered a diplomatic infection caught on learning that Edward did not mean to attend the wedding. To the two who were his deputies in peace as in war he assigned his role as host:

> the earl Thomas
> And the good lord too of Douglas
> In-till his stead ordained he
> Devisers of the feast to be.

It was they who accompanied the little prince to Berwick, who received there his bride and the English notables led by Isabelle and Mortimer who escorted her, and who on 17 July looked on as the boy of four and the girl of seven were joined in the union that was to prove as barren personally as politically.

The concomitant festivities afforded the English and Scottish leaders a chance of informal consultation on matters of common interest. Among these must have been the shelved problem of the 'disinherited', and it may have been now that Douglas raised with Isabelle or Mortimer the question of Faudon's restoration. That he should have pressed for this is surprising. He had no interest in Faudon as a possession, and no one can have been better acquainted with Robert's objection to the restitution of estates across national allegiances; and though Douglas was probably unique among the disinherited in that, since Bannockburn at least, he must through his ascendancy in Northumberland have controlled the disputed estate for long periods, its formal re-grant to him certainly would not strengthen Robert's case for opposing general restoration. That he nevertheless pursued his aim suggests that here he was obeying an older loyalty even than to the king, and that he had in fact once literally vowed to regain all his father had lost. He was eventually to succeed; on 12 May 1329, Edward III issued a charter restoring to Douglas the manor of Faudon in Northumberland, and all other lands in England forfeited by his father, 'by the King's special favour'. James thereupon bestowed the estate on his brother Archibald.

The wedding festivities over, Douglas and Moray, before

taking the baby pair to Robert at his palace at Cardross, performed a final act of courtesy by accompanying Isabelle and her train some distance into England on her way home. The country they traversed would have been unrecognizable to Alexander III. Where he had known villages, only green humps marked habitations that had returned to the earth from which they were made. Nettles flourished in what had been tofts raising a family's vegetables, and the diminishing pasture where cattle and geese had once grazed was cropped by the occasional deer. To Douglas this must have been the normal aspect of the land. He was a foreigner to peace, a state unknown here since his childhood, and the wilderness he saw probably seemed to him a frontier's natural condition. If so he was, for this frontier, right. In Alexander's day men living within reach of the Border could sow in expectation of reaping, but three hundred years would pass thereafter before the confidence torn up by Edward I could take root again.

King Robert had at last obtained the objectives with which he seized his crown. Scotland was free and independent, his own regality accepted throughout Europe, and the final goal was reached in October when the Pope lifted his excommunication from king and kingdom. All Robert now lacked was health to enjoy this fruition, still suffering as he was from the unidentified illness that had afflicted him at intervals for well over a year. This ailment, whatever it was, does not seem to have been looked on as potentially mortal (and may not indeed have been the proximate cause of his death), for as late as the spring of 1329 the regent-designate, Moray, was contemplating foreign travel;* on 17 April Edward III issued a safe-conduct for the earl's passage through England on his way abroad.

A little earlier, towards the end of March, Robert set out from Cardross on a pilgrimage to Whithorn in Galloway, the cradle of Scottish Christianity. With him went Douglas, now it seems seldom absent from the king. The royal procession moved slowly southward through Kyle, past the hills where Robert and James had fought the skirmishes and lurked in the hideouts of their outlaw days twenty-two years before, and down to southern Galloway to reach the shores of Luce Bay at the end of March. There before continuing to Whithorn they visited Myroch, near

* His purpose may have been to carry to Avignon Robert's plea for papal approval of the anointing of the King of Scots.

where lay the well of St Modenna, reputed, as was St Ninian's shrine, to possess healing powers. But if this pilgrimage represented a quest for health, it was unavailing. The king's condition rapidly deteriorated, and before many weeks had passed it grew plain that he had not long to live. At Cardross he made ready for his end. His will was drawn up, his estate ordered, the magnates of Scotland were summoned to do homage to his son and, having made his last dispositions for the state, Robert turned to his personal desire.

He long had dreamed that, when the war was ended and Scotland secure, he would go on crusade. Compassionate beyond most men of his time, he had never grown hardened to the suffering caused by war, or managed to acquit himself of a share in the blame for it; yet being still a product of his age, he could conceive no atonement for bloodshed but the shedding of more, non-Christian, blood. Almost to the end, it seems, he had hoped that he might yet achieve his dream; he was now fifty-four and by contemporary standards an old man, but his grandfather had gone crusading at sixty. Now at last relinquishing the hope, he had devised a means of participating after his death in its realization by another, a surrogate who should carry with him to war against the infidel the heart that had longed to pursue that contest.* That other, if Robert might have his wish, would be Douglas. He may nevertheless have sensed the folly of sending out of Scotland and into peril the man who, himself gone, would be the country's first soldier and second statesman, for according to Barbour he did not at first admit to this desire. Instead, summoning a group of councillors, he told them of his dream, now attainable only by proxy, of expiating his misdeeds on crusade, and asked them to nominate the knight who, bearing his heart, should war against Christ's enemies in his stead. Possibly he gave them, consciously or unconsciously, some hint of the answer he desired. At any rate they returned it; no man was as fit for such a charge as the lord Douglas. Happily confessing that all along it had been Douglas he longed to name, the king summoned his friend to the interview that was to be unmatchably described by Froissart (Lord Berners' translation).

* Had Robert conceived this idea earlier, he would presumably have sought a papal dispensation for the mutilation of his body; Moray applied for this retrospectively.

He called to him the gentle knight Lord James Douglas, and said before all the lords: 'Lord James, my dear friend, you know well that I have had much ado in my days to uphold and sustain the right of this realm; and when I had most ado I made a solemn vow, the which as yet I have not accomplished, wherefor I am right sorry; the which was, if I might achieve and make an end of all my wars, so that I might once have brought this realm in rest and peace, then I promised in my mind to have gone and warred on Christ's enemies, adversaries to our holy Christian faith. To this purpose mine heart hath ever intended, but our Lord would not consent thereto; for I have had so much ado in my days, and now in my last enterprise I have taken such a malady as I cannot escape. And sith it is so, that my body cannot go nor achieve that my heart desireth, I will send the heart instead of the body to accomplish mine avow. And because I know in all my realm no knight more valiant than ye be, nor of body so well furnished to accomplish mine avow instead of myself, therefore I require you, mine own dear especial friend, that ye will take on you this voyage, for the love of me, and to acquit my soul against my Lord God. For I trust so much in your nobleness and truth, that an ye will take it on you I doubt not but that ye shall achieve it, and declare then shall I die in more ease and quiet so that it be done in such manner as I shall declare unto you. I will that as soon as I am trespassed out of this world, that ye take my heart out of my body, and embalm it, and take of my treasure as you shall think sufficient for that enterprise, both for yourself and such company as ye will take with you, and present my heart to the Holy Sepulchre where our Lord lay,[*] seeing my body cannot come there; and take with you such company and purveyance as shall be appertaining to your estate. And wheresoever ye come, let it be known how ye carry with you the heart of King Robert

---

[*] Here Froissart erred: a letter from David II to Melrose Abbey refers to Robert's wish that his heart be buried there, as eventually it was. From the accounts of Barbour and Le Baker, and the terms of the papal absolution for the mutilation of the body, it appears that Robert's request was that his heart be borne in battle against the heathen and carried on pilgrimage to the Holy Sepulchre before its ultimate burial at home.

of Scotland, at his instance, to be presented to the Holy Sepulchre.'

Then all the lords that heard these words wept for pity; and when this knight Lord James Douglas might speak for weeping, he said, 'Ah, gentle and noble king, a hundred times I thank your grace of the great honour that ye do to me, sith of so great and noble a treasure ye give me in charge; and, sir, I shall do with a glad heart all that ye have commanded me, to the best of my true power, howbeit I am not worthy nor sufficient to achieve such a noble enterprise.' Then the king said, 'Ah, gentle knight, I thank you, so that ye will promise to do it.' 'Sir,' said the knight, 'I shall do it undoubtedly by the faith that I owe to God and to the order of knighthood.' 'Then I thank you,' said the king, 'for now shall I die in more ease of mind, sith that I know that the most worthy and sufficient knight of my realm shall achieve for me that which I could never attain unto.'

And thus soon after this noble Robert de Bruce King of Scotland trespassed out of this uncertain world in the year of our Lord God 1329, the seventh day of the month of June, and his heart was taken out of his body and embalmed, and honourably he was interred in the abbey of Dunfermline.

Chapter 11

The Last Commission

> I have a journey, sir, shortly to go;
> My master calls me,—I must not say no.
> Shakespeare

There was for Douglas no question of advancing a crusade on the soil of the Holy Land. Acre, the last foothold in Palestine of the crusading kingdom of Outremer, had been lost in 1291, and crusading energies had ever since been divided. In the Baltic the frontiers against the heathen Lithuanians were gradually being pushed forward in campaigns seldom shared by the French-speakers of the west, who felt themselves aliens there as they could not in the other theatres of crusading war. In the eastern Mediterranean, the devalued claims of the original crusaders were still nominally upheld in Rhodes, now the Hospitallers' base, and Cyprus, kingdom of the last dynasty of Outremer, and at the other end of the Mediterranean the halted advance of the Christians in Spain was recommencing and attracting to Castile adventurous knights from all over western Europe. It was Spain that Douglas chose as his first destination on Robert's behalf, though he may perhaps have intended to turn later to the service of the King of Cyprus on his way to the Holy Land that Christians now could enter only as pilgrims. He would have time enough, for he had determined to devote six or seven years to the enterprise; there would be nothing niggardly in his sacrifice for the good of Robert's soul. His decisions are evidenced by two letters. Edward III issued, obviously in answer to Douglas's request, on 1 September, one a safe-conduct in Edward's territories for seven years for James, lord of Douglas, on his way to the Holy Land with the heart of the late Robert, King of Scotland, in aid of the Christians against the Saracens, the other a commendation to Edward's cousin Alfonso XI of Castile, asking his favour towards Douglas who, 'burning with love of the Crucified', was about to set forth on this mission.*

Douglas now began to set his affairs in order, arranged the governance of his estates during his long absence, and made his will. This last, a measure advisable then for any traveller, was for him essential. Death in battle was only one of the hazards facing the crusader, disease representing, especially for northerners unacclimatized to the heat and infections of the south, an even greater risk, and Douglas must have known there was a strong chance he would never return to Scotland. His will does not survive, but the disposition of his estates is known. His elder son, William, was his heir.

It is not known whether Douglas ever married. His only other known child, Archibald, was certainly illegitimate, but it may be that William, who succeeded his father as lord of Douglas, was not. His succession is not in itself absolutely evidence of legitimacy, for in fourteenth-century Scotland a bastard inheriting estates might—as is shown by a later devolution of the Douglas heritage—assume the title that accompanied them, while if James had lacked a legitimate son his incentive to make a bastard his successor would have been a strong one, his natural heir being otherwise his brother Hugh, who even if not mentally defective was certainly incompetent to discharge the responsibilities of the lord of Douglas. William was by now probably in his middle teens (though referred to as lord of Douglas he seems never to have been formally invested with the title, which suggests that though old enough to bear arms he was still a minor when he died at Halidon Hill in 1334) and not too young for his father to form some opinion of his ultimate fitness for the inheritance. But the odds are he was born in wedlock. An adult unmarried baron would have been a rarity at this time, particularly in Robert Bruce's circle; Robert was a believer in marriage as a cement for political

* The letter to Alfonso disproves Froissart's statement that the idea of the expedition to Castile was conceived only while Douglas was at Sluys, which is apparently the basis of the enduring myth that Douglas allowed the prospect of fighting in Spain to divert him from his mission.

associations,* and as an eligible bachelor close to the king Douglas would have been an obvious candidate for the altar.

The identity of William's mother is unknown, and only a misstatement by Hume of Godscroft the seventeenth-century Douglas historian, suggests a possible direction for conjecture. Godscroft believed that the first wife of William le Hardi, and the mother of James, was the Marischal's sister Isabella Keith. In this he was certainly wrong; the evidence that James's mother was a Stewart is nearly contemporary and reliable.† The error, however, unlike most mis-statements of this Douglas hagiographer, does nothing to inflate the glory of the Douglases—rather the contrary, indeed, for even at the end of the thirteenth century a Stewart alliance outweighed a Keith one—and thus must represent what Godscroft and his source genuinely believed to be fact. There is also some slight ground for surmising a particular association between James of Douglas and Robert Keith the Marischal, who with James's cousin Walter the Steward, and except for the chancellor, witnessing *ex officio*, attested more of the surviving charters to or from James than any other witness. It is possible that Keith was James's uncle by marriage; his wife is said to have been a Barbara Douglas, of unknown parentage, who could have been an otherwise unrecorded sister of William le Hardi. But it is also possible that Godscroft was right in thinking that in the late thirteenth or early fourteenth century an Isabella Keith married a lord of Douglas, and wrong only in assigning her to the fourth and not the fifth lord; that she was the daughter and not the sister of the Marischal, the wife of James and the mother of his heir.

Archibald's mother, like his half-brother's, is beyond identification. She may have been a Ramsay of Dawolsey, for Froissart, who knew Archibald, believed Alexander Ramsay to be his cousin and no known Douglas–Ramsay or Stewart–Ramsay marriage would account for such a relationship. Almost certainly she was

* In the early years of the reign and after the recovery of Scotland began his available marriageable relatives were betrothed or married to the kin of nobles whose allegiance he wished to secure: his sister Matilda to the earl of Ross's heir and his brother Edward (with unhappy results) to the earl of Atholl's sister. A marriage between Douglas and a daughter of the Marischal would fit this pattern.

† Barbour, X, 727–8, and XI, 324. According to the *Liber Pluscardensis*, Robert II referred to Archibald the Grim as his cousin.

James's last lover, for her son must have been a baby when his father died, if indeed he was not posthumous; he first appears in history at the battle of Poitiers, twenty-six years after James's death, and then seems to have been reckoned a young man. For Archibald, apparently, no provision was made from his father's estates. He was to set out in life a landless youth, advantaged only by the recognition of the Douglases and by an upbringing befitting his father's son. The material benefit he was ultimately to derive from his paternity resulted from no act of James's but from the formal resignation of the barony and properties of Douglas by Hugh the Dull in 1342. David II's charter of re-grant, made 'in recognition of the fidelity, desert and valuable labours of James, late lord of Douglas, in the defence of our realm', entailed the inheritance first on William the son of Archibald Tineman—later first earl of Douglas—and his lawful heirs-male; failing them on William Douglas, 'the dark knight of Liddesdale', and *his* lawful heirs-male; and failing them on Archibald. Since the younger William was in any case natural heir to Hugh and the older merely a second cousin both to him and to James, the only clause in the grant that can be supposed a tribute to James's memory must be the inclusion in the entail of his illegitimate son. At that time, with two fertile males in line before Archibald, the provision can have seemed no more than a gesture, but the unlikely came about. The older William when he died at the hands of the younger left only a daughter, the younger's one legitimate son, the second earl, left no lawful male heir when he came to his celebrated end at Otterburn in 1388, and Archibald, claiming under the entail of 1342, succeeded to the vast estates that had been his father's and to the title of earl of Douglas.*

By then he had no need of them, his paternal inheritance having

---

* This succession, unusual even then (Froissart, speculating on the Douglas succession after Otterburn, supposed Archibald disqualified by his bastardy), later became so unthinkable as to make Archibald, despite the *Scotichronicon*'s explicit introduction of him as 'son of the most noble lord James, who afterwards was lord of Galloway and earl of Douglas', a great puzzle to historians. Their solution was to split him in two, James's bastard, and another, unplaceable but legitimate, Archibald who succeeded as third earl. He was ultimately reassembled by Sir William Fraser, who in *The Douglas Book* drew attention to the charter of 1342 and to a grant of land to the monastery of Holywood made by Archibald as earl of Douglas for the soul of his father, James, lord of Douglas.

THE LAST COMMISSION

after all sufficed. With his father's dark colouring and formidable strength ('Sir Archibald Douglas fought on foot', wrote Froissart of a Border skirmish, 'effortlessly wielding a sword two ells long, which an ordinary man could scarcely lift from the ground'), he inherited the brains and drive that had turned James from a penniless squire into regent-designate of Scotland in twelve years. By 1361 he was sheriff of Edinburgh and constable of its castle, by 1364 Scottish Warden of the West March. In 1369 David II created him lord of Galloway, 'because he took great travail to purge the country of English blood', and in 1372 he bought Wigtown together with its earldom from its then holder Thomas Fleming, who found the turbulent Gallovidians beyond his control. They were not beyond Archibald's. He broke them to his bridle, codified their laws and welded the separatist province at last firmly into the kingdom of Scotland. The landless bastard was to die a double earl, the greatest non-royal subject in Scotland, rumoured refuser of the first Scottish dukedom offered outside the royal family, with his daughter married to the king's son and his sons to the daughters and grand-daughters of kings.

While Douglas was preparing his crusade there occurred an event which, then trivial, appeared to the Scots to have grave repercussions later. A man called Twynam Lowrison, probably a Gallovidian, was rebuked for loose living by William of Eckford, an official of the diocese of Glasgow, took offence, kidnapped William and screwed a sizeable ransom out of him. This crime was reported to Douglas, who gave orders for Lowrison's arrest. Learning of this and realizing that the efficiency of Douglas's officers and the firmness of the baron's justice boded ill for himself, Lowrison left the country for the Picardy estate of Edward Balliol, son of the late ex-king John, and when two years later Edward returned to Scotland under arms to seek his father's crown, the Scots ascribed his act to Lowrison's prompting. Since Edward Balliol had already been invited to England by Edward III, and was in 1331 visited by Henry Beaumont, leader of the English 'disinherited', intent on persuading him to assert his rights, the advice of an obscure Scotsman is unlikely to have determined his decision, but it could be that Lowrison encouraged him with assurances—justified as far as Galloway was concerned—that some Scots would welcome the return of John Balliol's son.

By the spring of 1330 Douglas had completed his preparations both material and spiritual. His last recorded act in Scotland—which is also his sole recorded donation to the church—was a grant, made at Douglas on 1 February, St Bride's day, of half the land of the manor of Kilmad to the Abbey of Newbattle (which already possessed the other half) on condition that annually on that day a mass be sung in honour of St Bride, and thirteen poor people fed, that the saint might intercede for his soul with God. Soon after he set sail from Berwick* with the companions of his undertaking. Of these the knights known to have accompanied him were William Sinclair of Roslin (awarded an annual pension of £40 from the Exchequer in recognition of his expected services in this mission) and his brother John, William Keith of Galston, and Robert and Walter Logan. None as far as is known was Douglas's vassal, but all were Lowlanders, men who had probably long followed his banner in battle and who may now have attended it on crusade out of devotion less to the cross than to their captain; this was certainly the case with Keith, who adored him. They sailed first to Sluys, where Douglas hoped to pick up news of actions against the Saracens, and there, briefly, stayed.

Douglas had no great taste for the display then almost obligatory on great men, but he could when he wished comport himself *en prince* and now, in discharge perhaps of his role as Robert's surrogate, he kept a state that impressed even the wealthy Flemings.

> He stayed at Sluys twelve days before he left [wrote Le Bel], and all the time would not set foot ashore, but remained upon his ships, and bore himself magnificently with kettledrums and trumpets, as though he had been the King of Scotland. And in his company he had a banneret and six other of the most valiant knights in Scotland, and twenty of the finest young squires in the country, not counting the rest of his entourage; and all his vessels, pots, basins, ewers, flagons, dishes, barrels, everything, were made of silver; and all men of rank who visited him there he feasted with two kinds of wine and two of spices.

* Barbour. Froissart says Montrose but, leaving aside the probability that Barbour's sources were more reliable here, it is unlikely that an expedition all known members of which were Lowlanders would march up to Angus to embark at a port much farther from their destination than Berwick.

THE LAST COMMISSION

From Sluys Douglas turned westward to Castile. The weather was stormy and his fleet coasted the shore, as most ships did when they could in those almost compassless days, probably making frequent landfalls. One of these was evidently at Santander, where Douglas did go ashore, to make an impression five centuries could not quite efface. During the Carlist wars in Spain last century, a visitor to the Basque general Dorregaray had pointed out to him a large grey stone which, Dorregaray said, was a memorial of 'a great warrior called El Duglas, who came long ago to fight the infidels in Spain'.*

Coasting Galicia and Portugal, they came at last to the stretch of coast held by Castile between Portugal and the kingdom of Granada, which alone survived of Moslem Andalusia after the Christian advances of the twelfth and early thirteenth centuries. The Reconquest had lost its impetus before Granada could be overwhelmed, and in the past half-century the Granadians, reinforced by the fierce troops of Morocco under the dynasty of the banu-Merin, had been striving to roll it back, their efforts benefiting from the internal disruptions in Castile that had resulted from long royal minorities. Alfonso XI of Castile had, however, reached his majority in 1327, at the age of seventeen, and at once had resumed his ancestors' task of forwarding the Reconquest, thus attaching to his service many of the footloose knights who still roamed Europe, ever ready for the excitements and profits of war and all the readier when to these was added a chance of eternal salvation.

Disembarking at Seville, where Alfonso had been wintering after a season of success both by land and sea, Douglas sent the young king word of his coming and his purpose, and soon was summoned and welcomed. Even without Edward's letter of commendation he would probably have found a warm welcome. In an age that still esteemed prowess in battle above all other secular attributes, Douglas's exploits had made him one of the most famous men living, while the mission that brought him overseas had captured imaginations beyond his native land. The foreign knights gathered in Castile flocked to his lodging to see him, prominent among them Englishmen eager to meet the man who so long had frustrated their own captains and ready, some of them, themselves to follow his three-starred banner.

* Introduction to vol. iii of *CDS*. The episode was described to Bain by Dorregaray's visitor, count Edward d'Albanie.

One of these visits led to an episode oddly illustrative of the attitudes and speech of the day. Among the English knights curious to see Douglas was one whose name is now unknown but who was 'held so wonder wight [strong]'

> That for one of the good was he
> Prized of all the Christianty.

His face proclaimed his military experience, being chequered with scars, a feature not only usual among veteran soldiers at a time when the face alone might in battle be unprotected by armour, but esteemed as evidence of valour. This man had so little doubt of finding the Scottish hero likewise battered that at the sight of Douglas's unblemished countenance he blurted out his amazement that so famous and experienced a knight should have no scar on his face. Douglas's quiet answer, 'God be praised, I always had hands to defend my head', greatly impressed its hearers once they had worked it out, not only by its gentleness but, Barbour tells us, by its subtlety. Even so slight an obliquity as this was plainly unusual in an age habituated only to straightforward, if sometimes ceremoniously elaborated, expression, and Barbour, writing for as sophisticated a lay audience as fourteenth-century Scotland could boast, thought it advisable after quoting Douglas's remark to paraphrase it, lest through the delicacy of its making his correction of the scar-faced knight be not apprehended.

The Castilians had decided that the objective of this year's campaigning should be the strongly fortified Moorish town of Teba de Hardales, dominating a stretch of country that with its castles could be expected to fall to Alfonso if the town were captured. A move against Teba had the further advantage that the town lay sufficiently near Christian territory for a besieging army to be supplied from Cordova and Ecija, both now Castilian towns. To Teba accordingly Alfonso marched, probably in July, with his army, the five hundred Portuguese knights under the Master of Christus who had been lent by his brother-in-law the king of Portugal (and were later withdrawn), and his foreign volunteers. The Christians pitched camp outside Teba, the town was encircled by siege-works, catapults and mangonels were brought up, and the siege began.

The King of Granada was a minor and a nonentity, but his powers were wielded by the greatest and most experienced of

Granadian soldiers, Osmin, a general with years of successes against the Christians behind him. On learning of the investment of Teba, Osmin at once assembled the Granadian levies and set out to relieve the town. He did not at once offer battle, but pitched camp at Turron, about three leagues distant from Teba on the other side of the Guada Teba river, which ran about half a league from the town. There for some days he remained without moving to attack the Christian army, which continued to batter the walls of Teba without interference save from the town's inhabitants, who on one occasion managed in a successful sally to burn a siege tower the Castilians had just completed. Osmin's men, however, constantly harried the Christians at the river when they drew water, till Alfonso gave orders that a daily guard be mounted on the bank.

On 26 August these guards reported that the Moors were massing beyond the Guada Teba, and plainly intended an attack. Alfonso's excellent intelligence service had however already notified him that Osmin himself with half his army had moved to a concealed position in a valley near the Christian camp, information that left little room for doubt that the advance to the river was a diversionary movement aimed at drawing out the Christian army and leaving their camp and siege equipment exposed to an attack by Osmin and his troop. The young king therefore held the main Christian force, armed, mounted and ready for battle, in its position, and directed a troop of knights and foot-soldiers under Don Pero Ferrandez de Castro, with the foreign auxiliaries, to repel the Moors at the river crossing. Don Pero set out and with him Douglas, the foreign knights at his back. Clustering about him were the knights of Scotland, all but William Keith whom a broken arm kept from action, and about his neck, in the enamelled silver casket he had had made for it, hung the embalmed heart of Robert Bruce.*

As the Christians charged upon them the Moors coming up from the river withdrew, obedient to their instructions, across it. The Christians, crossing after them, kept on with undiminished momentum to drive at the Moors in a fierce onslaught that carried both forces back towards Turron. Osmin, meanwhile, hearing the sounds of battle and supposing the first phase of his

* The famous story of the Throwing of the Heart appears to be a fifteenth-century invention; see Appendix 1.

operation to be well under way, led his own troop out of concealment and towards the Christian camp, only to see it bristling with armed men while on the other side of the river the feigned withdrawal of his diversionary force was turning into a real rout. At once abandoning his plans, he hastened to the aid of his men, now falling back as far as their own camp, and Alfonso, seeing Don Pero's troops engaged by the whole Moorish army, in his turn dispatched reinforcements to the attacking Christians.

Charging with uncharacteristic impetuosity, Douglas had penetrated far into the Moorish ranks. Realizing evidently that he had outdistanced the Castilians, he checked and began, attended by the handful of Scots, the Logans among them, who had kept at his side, to forge a way back towards Don Pero's men. One Scot, however, had become separated even from this small group, William Sinclair of Roslin, cut off and surrounded by a host of Saracens, and with his companions Douglas turned aside to go to Sinclair's rescue. The attempt was vain, and to its makers fatal.

It was said of Douglas that he engaged in seventy battles and in fifty-seven prevailed. His last was among the victories. Osmin's support came too late to save his army, and though not yet wholly driven from the field it was rendered by this day's fighting incapable of further effort to save Teba. The town was to fall a few days later.

Douglas's body, pierced by five mortal wounds, was found in a ring of dead Moors by his men as they searched the battlefield. Lamenting like men gone mad, they took it up and carried it to his tent. They had more cause for lamentation than they knew. This romantic, wasteful death would prove catastrophic for Scotland. When Douglas died Moray had less than two years to live, within months of his death the war with England would break out afresh, and Scotland, deprived of the regent who should have led and defended her, would re-experience at the hands of Edward III all she had undergone from Edward I. Yet for Douglas himself it is questionable if longer life would have brought greater satisfaction. Few mediaeval and fewer Scottish regents came to happy ends. Dying when he did, he never knew how brief the long-striven-for peace would prove. He was spared the need to take up again, alone and ageing, the struggle he had waged young and greatly companioned, spared seeing how Robert's son would turn out, spared the decline of age and sickness.

THE LAST COMMISSION

With the tasks life had set him completed, he died, as he would surely have wished, in battle; he had always been lucky, in his time, his country, his king, and he may at the last have been lucky in his death.

The bones of Douglas, the flesh boiled off them in obedience to the grim sentimentality that decreed burial in his own land, were brought home to Scotland, with Bruce's heart, by William Keith of Galston. They lie in Douglasdale, in the church of St Bride.

Appendix 1

The Myth of the Thrown Heart

Possibly the best-known story concerning James of Douglas is that which relates how, cut off by the Moors and knowing he had no chance of survival, he threw the heart of Bruce ahead of him into the Moorish hosts and charged after it shouting, 'Go first as thou was wont to do and Douglas will follow thee or die'. This romantic tale is almost certainly fictitious. Of the chroniclers nearest in time to Douglas, not one mentions it; it makes its first appearance in the fifteenth century.

Four fourteenth-century chroniclers recorded the death of Douglas in some detail: Le Bel, Froissart, Geoffrey Le Baker, and of course Barbour. All knew of Robert's last commission to him, and that the heart of Bruce must therefore have been with him at the time of his death, and not one mentions the 'throwing'.

Le Bel describes how Douglas and those with him, advancing too far into the Saracen host, were cut off and killed to a man, but says nothing of any demonstration with the heart. Froissart, who, as has been said, drew his accounts of the deaths of Robert and Douglas from Le Bel, had sources of information not available to Le Bel. He knew the first earl of Douglas, whom indeed he looked on as his patron in Scotland (as he tells his readers more than once, he was for a fortnight the earl's guest at his castle of Dalkeith), and also appears to have known James's son, Archibald the Grim. But if any tradition of the throwing of the heart was preserved in the Douglas family, Froissart never learned of it; it is inconceivable that this lover of the dramatic utterance and the flamboyant gesture would have failed to introduce such an episode into his chronicle had he known of it.

Geoffrey Le Baker, an English contemporary of Le Bel's, gives in his *Chronicon* a short account of Douglas's death which is of particular interest in that he alone of the chroniclers to record it identifies the source of his information. This was a Carmelite friar, Thomas de Lavington, who while still a layman had fought under Douglas in Spain,

APPENDIX I

and thus must have been at the siege of Teba. Le Baker says nothing of the heart's being thrown.

Nor does *The Bruce*, in those manuscripts which can be relied on as representing what Barbour wrote, mention the incident. It is, however, probably to the inclusion of additional matter in the first printed edition of *The Bruce* that the legend owes its longevity.

The Bruce survives in two fifteenth-century manuscripts by different hands, one at Cambridge and one at Edinburgh. The first part (up to September 1306) of the Cambridge manuscript is missing, but in the preponderant part of *The Bruce* which is recorded in both manuscripts the correspondence between the two is close, the occasional variation being no more than can be accounted for by scribal error. What appears in both the manuscripts can therefore be accepted as what Barbour wrote. The account they give of Douglas's death is, as might be expected, the fullest to survive; Barbour alone, for instance, mentions the cutting off of William Sinclair and Douglas's effort to rescue him, an important point as explaining in part the uncharacteristic rashness that led to the death of Douglas. He also mentions that Douglas had the heart of Bruce hanging round his neck when he rode into battle; but says nothing of its being thrown ahead.

In 1571, however, the first printed edition of *The Bruce* appeared, and this, and other early printed editions of the chronicle which apparently were based on it, contain lines and passages which do not appear in either of the manuscripts. One of these additional passages, inserted before the account of Douglas's death, runs:

> But ere they joined in battell,
> What Douglas did, I sall you tell.
> The Bruce's heart, that on his breast
> Was hanging, in the field he kest
> Upon a stone-cast and well more:
> And said: 'Now pass thou forth before,
> As thou wast wont in field to be,
> And I sall follow, or else die.'
> And so he did withouten ho [delay],
> He fought ever while he came it to,
> And took it up in great dantee [honour];
> And ever in field thus used he.

Despite its absence from the manuscripts and the extreme improbability of the same (or indeed any) lengthy passage having been omitted in each of two independent copyings of Barbour's work, this passage was long accepted as authentic. One reason for this acceptance was that the passage closely resembled one in *The Buke of the Howlat*, a laudatory verse account of the Douglas family written in the mid fifteenth century,

APPENDIX I

which was assumed to be an independent recording of a genuine tradition. In the nineteenth century, however, P. Buss, drawing attention to the appearance in the passage of verbal forms not usual in Barbour's unquestioned work, suggested that it was an interpolation, and F. J. Amours, the editor of *The Buke of the Howlat*, opined that the passage about the throwing of the heart in that work was the source of the interpolation. This conclusion was considered and accepted by W. M. Mackenzie in his definitive edition of *The Bruce*.

Another point worth noting about the 'throwing of the heart' passage in the early printed editions of *The Bruce* is that in it Douglas is made to address the heart—and thus, symbolically, Robert—as 'thou'. But in all conversations between Robert and Douglas related in the manuscripts of *The Bruce*, Douglas addresses the king as 'you', and is addressed as 'thou'. This supports the assumption that, while Barbour wrote at a time when the correct social uses of the second persons singular and plural were still understood, the interpolated passage was composed at a later date, when they had been forgotten.

One last hypothesis remains to be noted. This is that the account of the 'throwing' in *The Buke of the Howlat* records an event which had actually occurred, and the memory of which had been orally preserved in the Douglas household. No such assumption is viable. While it certainly is not impossible for a historic event to be preserved in oral tradition alone for a century or more, this is most unlikely to happen with a dramatic episode concerning an event which in the meantime has been described in writing several times. Any premiss that the 'throwing of the heart' really happened but was not recorded in writing until the mid fifteenth century entails the acceptance of every one of a number of separate and unlikely assumptions. These are: that Barbour, who knew Archibald the Grim and who certainly would have made every effort to gather and record information about the death of his second hero, never heard of the episode; that Le Bel never heard of it, or if he did thought it not worth mentioning; that Froissart, despite his acquaintance with the Douglases, never heard of it; and that either Lavington (who must have known of any such episode had it occurred and been witnessed) thought it less worth mentioning to Le Baker than the number of mortal wounds sustained by Douglas, or Le Baker, although told of it, thought it not worth recording. The failure of all these chroniclers to mention any such episode renders untenable the hypothesis that the tale of the 'throwing' represents fact, and leaves little room for doubt that the story was invented, either by the author of *The Buke of the Howlat* or by some other glorifier of Douglas family tradition.

Appendix 2

Genealogy of the Douglas Family in the Thirteenth and Fourteenth Centuries

APPENDIX 2

William 'Longleg', m. Constance
lord of Douglas,
born *c.* 1200, died before 1274

- Willelma, m. William Galbraith of Dalserf
  died 1302
  - Joan, m.-de Cathe
    - Bernard

- Hugh, m. Marjorie (? lord of Douglas) of Abernethy, born *c.* 1240, died before 1288
  - Elizabeth (1) m. William 'le Hardi', m. (2) Eleanor de Lovaine, widow of William Ferrers
    Stewart   lord of Douglas,
               born *c.* 1245,
               died in the Tower
               1298
    - ? m. James 'the Black', 'the Good', lord of Douglas, born *c.* 1286, killed at Teba de Hardales 1330
      - William, lord of Douglas, born *c.* 1315, killed at Halidon Hill 1334
    - Hugh 'the Dull', lord of Douglas, born 1294, died *c.* 1347
      - Archibald 'the Grim' lord of Galloway, earl of Wigtown 3rd earl of Douglas, born *c.* 1330, died 1400
        - Black Douglases

APPENDIX 2

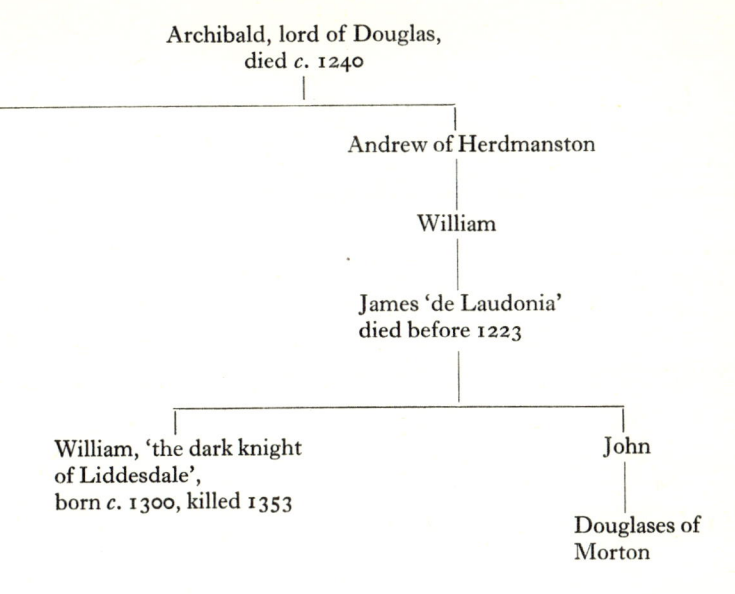

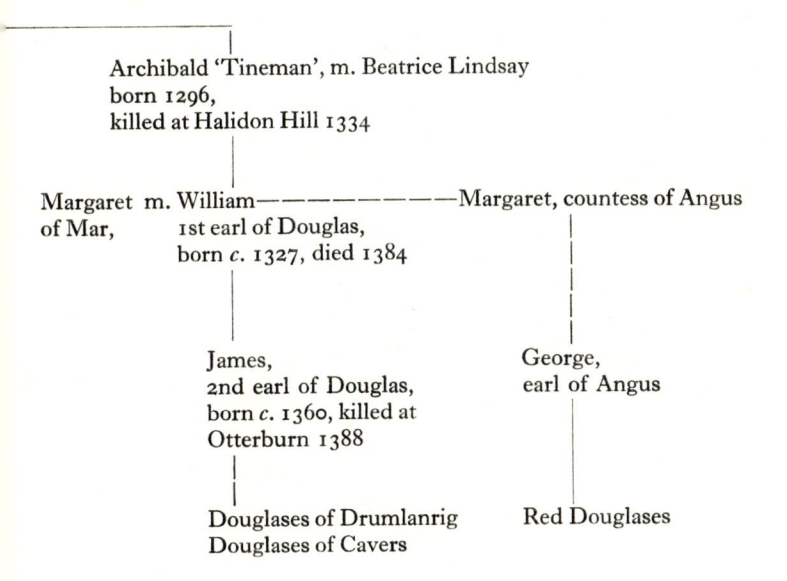

Archibald, lord of Douglas, died *c.* 1240
├── Andrew of Herdmanston
│   │
│   William
│   │
│   James 'de Laudonia' died before 1223
│   ├── William, 'the dark knight of Liddesdale', born *c.* 1300, killed 1353
│   └── John
│   │
│   Douglases of Morton
│
└── Archibald 'Tineman', m. Beatrice Lindsay, born 1296, killed at Halidon Hill 1334
    │
    Margaret m. William ———————— Margaret, countess of Angus
    of Mar,   1st earl of Douglas,
               born *c.* 1327, died 1384
    ├── James, 2nd earl of Douglas, born *c.* 1360, killed at Otterburn 1388
    │   │
    │   Douglases of Drumlanrig
    │   Douglases of Cavers
    └── George, earl of Angus
        │
        Red Douglases

Sources

Note on quotations

All verse quotations in the text, except 'Good King Robert's Testament' on page 39 (an anonymous translation of an anonymous Latin rhyme quoted in the *Scotichronicon*), are from *The Bruce*; they have been modernized in spelling and, where this seems desirable for clarity, in language.

Scottish chronicles

The most important source of information on Douglas's career, and for a number of episodes in it the only one, is Barbour's verse chronicle *The Bruce*.

John Barbour, who was probably born in the later years of Robert Bruce's reign, and who became archdeacon of Aberdeen, completed *The Bruce* about 1376. He explained in the preamble to his narrative his purposes in writing it: to tell a story that should combine with the attractions of the popular romances of the day the further attraction of being true, and in so doing to record, that their great deeds should not be forgotten, the achievements of Robert Bruce and James of Douglas. About his methods of research Barbour says little, merely referring at times to items of information as having been given him by survivors of the period he records (he mentions, for instance, that the appearance of Douglas was described to him by people who remembered the hero), but it is known from statements made by Gray and Le Bel (see below) that there existed in the mid-fourteenth-century Scottish chronicles written in Robert's reign which have not survived, and there can be little doubt that Barbour also drew on these. The result is of great value. Though Barbour sometimes, possibly for artistic reasons, relates events out of their chronological order, and though he is sometimes inaccurate in his sketching of the events that led up to the war and in the narrative summaries that link the episodes he describes so vividly, comparison with other chronicles of the period and with the documents surviving from it has shown that he is in the main to be relied upon, and in detail is often remarkably accurate.

Barbour's contemporary, John Fordun, had compiled notes for a chronicle of Scotland covering the War of Independence (recording in them the date of Douglas's death, which Barbour does not mention), and in the fifteenth century these were expanded by Walter Bower, with a continuation up to his own time, into the *Scotichronicon*. Both Bower and the rather earlier Scottish chronicler Andrew Wyntoun, author of the *Origynall Chronikyl of Scotland*, felt, however, that the reign of Robert I had been so admirably recorded by Barbour that there was no point in dealing with the themes he had handled, and their work therefore adds comparatively little to the material on this period or to knowledge about Douglas.

Other chronicles

Of the much more numerous English chronicles written or continued in the fourteenth century, two are of especial importance for the Scottish War of Independence: the *Lanercost Chronicle* and Sir Thomas Gray's *Scalacronica*.

The *Lanercost Chronicle* was probably written at the priory of the Minorites at Lanercost, near Carlisle. References in it to matters personally known to or witnessed by the chronicler (or successive chroniclers) suggest that the events it relates were usually recorded as or soon after they occurred. It was natural for monastic chroniclers to pay especial attention to affairs in their own neighbourhood, and the Lanercost chroniclers were no exception; this chronicle gives very full details of events on the Border and of Scottish incursions into England, and its account of the siege of Carlisle in 1315 is the most comprehensive we have.

Sir Thomas Gray of Heaton in Northumberland was unusual among mediaeval chroniclers in being a soldier. The son of a knight who had been constantly engaged in the War of Independence, and himself active in the renewed Anglo-Scottish wars in the reign of Edward III, Gray was captured by the Scots in 1355 and wrote his *Scalacronica* as a prisoner in Edinburgh Castle where, he relates, there were kept Scottish chronicles both in verse and in prose, of which he made use. As might be expected, Gray is particularly informative about the effects of the war on Northumberland, and especially about events there in the years after Bannockburn, and in 1327. His account of Bannockburn—which his father witnessed as a prisoner with the Scots, having been captured in the fight between Clifford's and Moray's divisions the previous day—is also interesting.

Though no other fourteenth-century English chroniclers were as directly concerned with the events of the war, most relate something of it or of episodes in it. The fourteenth-century continuators of the *Brut* chronicle and of *Flores Historiarum*, the author of *Vita Edwardi Secundi*, the Melsa and Bridlington chroniclers, Walter of Guisborough, Murimuth, Trokelowe, Geoffrey Le Baker, Knighton and Walsingham all record material of interest here, Guisborough's chronicle being of especial importance for the early years of the war and the *Vita Edwardi Secundi* for the reign of Edward II up to 1326. Most of these chroniclers describe the battle of Bannockburn, and the Scottish recapture and English siege of Berwick are referred to by several. The Chapter of Myton also receives a great deal of attention, possibly because the role played in it by clerics rendered it peculiarly interesting to clerical writers; the accounts in *Vita Edwardi Secundi* and in the *Brut* and Bridlington chronicles are particularly detailed. The excommunication of Douglas and Moray by name in 1318 is mentioned in the *Brut* chronicle. The unsuccessful English invasion of Scotland in 1322 and the subsequent battle of Byland are dealt with by most of the English chroniclers, Trokelowe being particularly informative about the effects on the English army of the lack of food in Scotland. Most also record the Weardale campaign of 1327, all these accounts, however brief, mentioning Douglas's night raid, which clearly made a great impression, though only Knighton refers to Douglas's passing himself off as an Englishman; it is also Knighton who records Douglas's treatment of captured English archers. An interesting account of the Scottish escape from Weardale also appears in the chronicle of John Hardyng; though Hardyng wrote in the early fifteenth century, he was a northerner, and may have drawn on earlier local accounts of events here. Murimuth, a clerk in the households of Edward II and Edward III, is the chronicler who identifies Douglas as the Scottish envoy to the Parliament of York in 1328.

The most important source of information on the Weardale campaign is the chronicle of Jean Le Bel, who took part in it on the English side. Le Bel wrote his chronicle some thirty years later; he explains that in preparing it he consulted other survivors (including Jean of Hainault) of the events he describes, and he also consulted written sources, referring to 'a book this good King Robert had made'. Though there are some minor discrepancies between Le Bel's account of the campaign and Barbour's (for instance, as to the lapse of time between the Scots' move to Stanhope Park and Douglas's night raid), and each mentions incidents not recorded by the other, the two narratives in general bear each other out well. A point worth noting is that the clerical chroniclers'

SOURCES

allegation that the English were 'betrayed' in Weardale (a charge of having 'betrayed' them was included in the indictment of Mortimer on his fall in 1330) receives no support from Le Bel, nor, significantly, is it mentioned by the other soldier-chronicler, Gray.

Another continental chronicle to refer to the life, or rather the death, of Douglas is *Les Grandes Chroniques de la France*. This is too full of inaccuracies—for instance, as to the circumstances in which Bruce's heart was committed to him, and the year of his death—to be relied upon, but is noteworthy as evidence of the interest his mission and death evoked in a country with which he had, as an adult, no connection.

The Castilian campaign of 1330 is described in the *Cronica del Rey Don Alfonso el Onceno*.

Records

Most of the documents surviving from the period are summarized in Joseph Bain's *Calendar of Documents Relating to Scotland*, vols ii and iii (abbreviated in the text to *CDS*). Among the documents relevant to Douglas's career are the letter mentioning his supposed thought of changing sides in May 1307; the letter from Edward II which alludes to the Foresters' change of allegiance in the autumn of 1307; the report of the Jedburgh monks' flight to England the day after he captured Roxburgh Castle; Maurice de Berkeley's reports to Edward III on the Gascons' ill-fated foray in 1316; William de Ros's claim for the losses he suffered in the Lintalee affray; Ralph Neville's petition for help with his ransom; Edward III's grant of Faudon to Douglas (Douglas's conveyance of the manor to his brother Archibald is recorded in *Calendar of Inquisitions Post Mortem*, vol. vii); and his safe-conduct and letter to Alfonso XI.

A number of documents concerning Scotland in the late thirteenth century, including those that bear on William of Douglas's abduction of Eleanor de Ferrers, his surrender in 1297, and his final imprisonment, are printed in Joseph Stevenson's *Documents Illustrative of the History of Scotland, 1286–1306*. Stevenson also printed, in *Illustrations of Scottish History from the Twelfth to the Sixteenth Century*, a short anonymous chronicle, probably written in the north, which gives the fullest account extant of the Lintalee affair as the English saw it, and an account of the Scottish recapture of Berwick.

Sir Francis Palgrave's *Documents and Records Illustrating the History of Scotland* prints numerous documents from the early part of the war, including those relating to William of Douglas's surrender, and Edward I's complaint to the Pope about Lamberton.

James of Douglas's letters to Thomas of Lancaster and to Ralph

SOURCES

Neville, and the safe-conducts he and Moray issued to Lancaster's agents, are printed in vol. 2 of Thomas Rymer's *Foedera, Conventiones, Literae*.

All the surviving charters to and from Douglas are printed in translation in vol. 3 of Sir William Fraser's *The Douglas Book*, and William Robertson's *Index of Charters* lists several other grants to him and to his kinsmen the charters of which have not survived. The Regency Act of 1318, the Declaration of Arbroath and the letters patent of March 1328 are printed in translation in *A Source-Book of Scottish History*, vol. i, edited by W. Croft Dickinson and others.

Bibliography

J. Bain: *Calendar of Documents Relating to Scotland* (London, 1881–8)
E. M. Barron: *The Scottish War of Independence* (Inverness, 1934)
G. W. S. Barrow: *Robert Bruce and the Community of the Realm of Scotland* (Eyre and Spottiswoode, 1965)
J. Conway Davies: *The Baronial Opposition to Edward III* (Cambridge, 1918)
William Croft Dickinson, Gordon Donaldson and Isabel Milne, eds: *A Source-Book of Scottish History*, vol. 1 (Nelson, 1952)
Sir William Fraser: *The Douglas Book* (1885)
David Hume of Godscroft: *History of the House of Douglas* (Edinburgh, 1743)
A. M. Mackenzie, ed.: *Scottish Pageant* (Edinburgh, 1946)
M. McKisack: *The Fourteenth Century* (Oxford, 1959)
Sir Herbert Maxwell: *History of the House of Douglas* (Freemantle, 1902)
J. E. Morris: *Bannockburn: A Centenary Monograph* (Cambridge University Press, 1914)
G. Neilson: 'The last journey of Robert Bruce', *Scottish Antiquary*, 1898
Ranald Nicholson: *Edward III and the Scots* (Oxford, 1965)
Sir Francis Palgrave, ed.: *Documents and Records Illustrating the History of Scotland* (London, 1837)
A. E. Price: 'The importance of the campaign of 1327', *English Historical Review*, 1935
W. Robertson: *Index of Charters granted by Sovereigns of Scotland, 1309–1413* (Edinburgh, 1798)
J. Scammell: 'Robert I and the north of England', *English Historical Review*, 1958
J. Stevenson, ed.: *Documents Illustrative of the History of Scotland 1286–1306* (Edinburgh, 1870)
J. Stevenson, ed.: *Illustrations of Scottish History from the Twelfth Century to the Sixteenth Century* (Maitland Club, 1834)
E. L. G. Stones: *Anglo-Scottish Relations, 1134–1328: Some Selected Documents* (Edinburgh, 1964)

BIBLIOGRAPHY

Documents and historical sources

Geoffrey le Baker: *Chronicon Angliae* (Caxton Society, 1847)
John Barbour: *The Bruce*, ed. W. M. Mackenzie (Black, 1909)
Jehan le Bel: *Les vrayes chroniques de Messire Jehan le Bel* (Brussels, 1863)
Canon of Bridlington: *Gesti Edwardi de Carnavan* (Rolls Series, 1883)
The *Brut* chronicle, ed. F. W. D. Brie (London, 1906)
Calendar of Inquisitions Post Mortem, and other documents in the Public Record Office (1904-12)
Cronica del Rey Don Alfonso el Onceno (Valladolid, 1551)
Vita Edwardi Secundi, ed. and trans. N. Denholm-Young (Nelson, 1957)
Exchequer Rolls of Scotland, ed. J. Stuart and others (Edinburgh, 1878-1908)
John Fordun: *Cronica Gentis Scotorum*, ed. W. F. Skene (Edinburgh, 1871-2)
John Fordun: *Scotichronicon cum Supplementis et Continuatione Walteri Boweri*, ed. W. Goodall (Edinburgh, 1757)
Jean Froissart: *Chroniques*, ed. Kervyn de Lettinhove (Brussels, 1863)
Les Grandes Chroniques de la France, ed. P. Paris (1836-8)
Sir Thomas Gray: *Scalacronica*, ed. and trans. Sir H. Maxwell (Glasgow, 1913)
Walter of Guisborough: *Chronica*, ed. H. Rothwell (London, 1957)
John Hardyng: *Chronicle* (1812)
Henry Knighton: *Chronicon* (Rolls Series, 1889-95)
Lanercost Chronicle, ed. and trans. Sir H. Maxwell (Glasgow, 1913)
Juan de Mariana: *Historia General de España* (1650)
Chronica de Melsa (Rolls Series, 1866-8)
Adam Murimuth: *Chronica sui temporis* (London, 1846)
Rotuli Scotiae in Turri Londinensi et in Domo Capitulari Asservati, ed. D. Macpherson and others, 1814-19
Thomas Rymer: *Foedera, Conventiones, Literae* (London, 1704-32)
Scots Peerage, ed. Sir J. Balfour Paul (Edinburgh, 1904-14)
John de Trokelowe: *Annales* (Rolls Series, 1866)
Thomas Walsingham: *Historia Brevis* (London, 1574)
Matthew of Westminster: *Flores Historiarum* (Rolls Series, 1890)
Andrew Wyntoun: *Orignyall Chronikyl of Scotland*, ed. D. Laing (Edinburgh, 1872-9)

Index

Abernethy, Laurence, lord of, 80-1
Alexander III, King of Scots, 1, 2, 7n, 51, 69, 101, 148, 149, 151
Alfonso XI, King of Castile, 156, 161-4, 175
Angus, John Stewart of Bonkle, earl of, 144
Angus, Robert Umfraville, earl of, 4, 110, 144n
Arbroath, Declaration of, 108-9, 114
Argyll, 49-51
Argyll, Alexander Macdowel, lord of, 23
Arundel, Edmund Fitzalan, earl of, 90-4
Atholl, David of Strathbogie, earl of, 38, 91, 110, 157n
Atholl, John of Strathbogie, earl of, 17, 22, 24, 27, 29, 38, 148
Ayreminne, William, 105

Badlesmere, Bartholomew, 111-12
Balliol, Edward, 34, 159
Balliol, Henry, 88
Balliol, John, lord of Galloway, King of Scots, 1, 2, 3, 10, 11, 14, 42, 45, 49n, 159
Bannockburn, battle of, 72-9, 82-3, 84, 104, 110, 128, 139, 173-4
Barbour, John, 4n, 26, 36n, 40n, 54, 55, 61n, 72n, 91, 94n, 95n, 117n, 118n, 135n, 137n, 140n, 152, 160n, 162, 166-8, 172-3
Beaumont, Henry, 72, 91, 159

Berkeley, Maurice, lord of, 87-8, 89, 175
Berwick, 11-12, 47, 57, 61, 67, 81, 87-8, 89, 96, 101, 125, 149-50, 160
massacre at, 2, 4
Scottish recapture of, 95, 98-100, 101
siege of, 103-4, 106
Bickerton, Walter, 56
Bohun, Henry, 74
Bohun, Humphrey, see Hereford
Bothwell Castle, 34, 58, 84-5
Bower, Walter, 173
Boyd, Robert, 22, 24, 26, 27-8, 34, 45
Brechin, David of, 45
Bridlington chronicler, 95n, 119-120, 174
Brittany, John of, see Richmond
Bruce, Alexander, dean of Glasgow, 17, 27, 29, 34
Bruce, Christian, 29, 85
Bruce, Edward, 17, 27, 42, 45-7, 59, 61-2, 65, 69, 70-1, 72, 75-7, 83-4, 157n
and kingship of Ireland, 85, 89, 99
death, 102
Bruce, Marjorie, 21, 27, 29, 84-5, 102
Bruce, Mary, 29, 85
Bruce, Matilda, 157n
Bruce, Nigel, 17, 21, 24, 27, 28
Bruce, Robert 'the Competitor', lord of Annandale, 1, 11

179

INDEX

Bruce, Robert, earl of Carrick, *see* Robert I
Bruce, Thomas, 17, 27, 29, 34
Brut chronicle, 95n, 130n, 139n, 174
Buchan, 45, 49, 124
Buchan, Isabel, countess of, 18, 21, 28-9
Buchan, John Comyn, earl of, 3, 18, 42, 44-5, 51
Byhrtnoth, 46-7
Byland, battle of, 117-19

Cailhau, Raymond, 88-9
Campbell, Neil, 22, 24-5
Carlisle, 29, 35, 38, 40
  siege of, 86-7, 173
Carlisle, earl of, *see* Harcla
Carrick, Robert Bruce, earl of, *see* Robert I
Cathe, Bernard, 30n, 39
Charles IV, King of France, 119, 127
Christiana of the Isles, 28
Clement V, Pope, 4n
Clifford, Robert, lord (father), 4, 5, 30, 31, 37, 40, 42-3, 72, 75, 77, 113
Clifford, Robert, lord (son), 113
Cobham, Ralph, 118
Comyn family, 3, 11, 14, 17, 18, 42, 45, 84
Comyn, John, lord of Badenoch, 11, 13-14, 20, 24, 30, 32, 84, 101n
Courtrai, battle of, 3, 76-7

David of Huntingdon, 11n
David, Prince, later David II, 147, 149, 150, 159
Denholm, William, 146
Despenser, Hugh, 111, 127-8
Dickson, Thomas, 31-3, 35
Douglas Castle, Lanarkshire, 33-4, 40, 42-3
Douglas, Archibald 'Tineman', 123-4, 134, 136, 139, 150, 158, 175

Douglas, Archibald 'the Grim', lord of Galloway, earl of Wigtown, 3rd earl of Douglas, 156, 157-9, 166, 168
Douglas, Eleanor, Lady, 4-5, 11, 16, 123, 175
Douglas, Hugh 'the Dull', lord of, 123, 156, 157
Douglas, James 'the Black', 'the Good', lord of, 4-5, 19, 20, 21, 29-30, 37, 38-9, 52, 57-8, 61, 69, 71-2, 101, 102, 108, 115-16, 117n, 121, 126, 127, 129, 146, 151, 155-6, 174, 175, 176
  character and appearance, 53-5
  parentage, 7
  evacuated to Paris, 8-9
  with Lamberton, 9-10, 13
  joins Robert Bruce, 16-17, 18
  on flight through Highlands, 22-26
  in Arran, 27-8
  and Douglas Larder, 31-5
  at Edryford, 36
  second attack on Douglas Castle, 40
  recaptures Douglas Castle, 42-3
  in the Forest, 43-5, 46-7
  and chivalry, 46-7, 137-8
  captures Thomas Randolph, 47-48
  at Pass of Brander, 49-50
  military attitudes and techniques, 36, 46, 60, 89, 136, 145
  captures Roxburgh Castle, 63-5
  at Bannockburn, 72-9
  pursuit of Edward II, 79-81, 82-3
  raids in northern England, 59, 83-4, 86, 107-8, 112, 130
  Warden of the Marches, 85-6, 94
  at siege of Carlisle, 86-7
  at Scaithmoor, 88-9
  joint Warden of Scotland, 89-90
  building of and combats at Lintalee, 90-4
  and subversion in England, 94-5, 113-14

INDEX

duel with Neville, 96-7
regent-designate, 102-3
partnership with Moray, 107, 112-14, 131, 137
and Chapter of Myton, 104-5
traffickings with Lancaster, 110, 112-14
at Byland, 117-19
estates, 122-3
and Weardale campaign, 107n, 131, 132-45, 174
ambassador to England, 147-9
and marriage of Prince David, 150-1
Robert I's last request to, 152-4
uncertainty whether married, 156-7
children, 156-9
at Sluys, 160-1
at Seville, 161-2
death, 163-5
alleged throwing of Bruce's heart, 166-8
Douglas, James, 2nd earl of, 158
Douglas, William 'le Hardi', lord of, 4-5, 7-9, 13, 100, 124, 149, 157, 175
Douglas, William 'the dark knight of Liddesdale', 123, 124, 158
Douglas, William, lord of, son of James, 123, 124, 156-7
Douglas, William, 1st earl of, 158, 166
Douglasdale, 11, 31-4, 42-3

Eckford, William of, 159
Edinburgh Castle, 47, 63, 65, 118n, 173
Edward I, King of England, 1-5, 7, 10, 11, 12, 18, 19, 20, 27, 29, 30, 34, 35, 38, 41, 47, 60, 83, 90, 108, 130, 149, 151, 164
Edward II, King of England, 12, 19, 41, 42, 49, 51, 82-3, 85, 87, 90, 94, 98, 109-10, 120, 121, 122, 130, 131n, 174, 175
invasion of Scotland (1310), 57-8
baronial opposition to, 54, 58, 62

preparations for 1314 campaign, 63, 66, 67-8, 71
at Bannockburn, 75-9
chased by Douglas, 79-81
and siege of Berwick, 103-4, 105
baronial rebellion against, 110-15
invasion of Scotland (1322), 115-117
flight from Byland, 119
enters into and violates truce, 122, 126
marital rebellion against, 127-8
deposition, 128, 129
Edward III, King of England, 127, 128, 130, 132, 134-7, 141, 145, 147, 148, 149, 150, 151, 155-6, 159, 164, 173, 174, 175
Elizabeth, Queen of Scots, 21, 27, 29, 85, 124
Ellis, a 'noble schavaldur', 93

Falkirk, battle of, 2, 44, 48, 68, 76
Faudon, 4, 7, 53, 124, 148, 150, 175
Fenes, Guillemin de, 64-5
Ferrandez de Castro, Pero, 163-4
Ferrers, Eleanor de, *see* Douglas, Eleanor
Fife, Duncan, earl of, 18, 108, 149
Fleming, Thomas, 159
Fordun, John, 173
Forest, the, 43-5, 57, 90, 92, 115-116, 123
Francis, William, 65
Fraser, Alexander, 56
Fraser, Simon, 15, 19, 29, 44, 148
Froissart, Jean, 132n, 152, 153n, 156n, 157, 158n, 159, 166, 168

Galloway, 41-2, 43, 45-6, 58, 61, 159
Gaveston, Piers, 54, 57-8, 62, 111, 115
Gilbertson, Walter, 84-5
Gloucester, Gilbert de Clare, earl of, 57, 68, 69, 77-8
Gordon, Adam, lord of, 47-8, 62-3, 88
Gray, Thomas, 56, 100

INDEX

Gray, Thomas, author of *Scalacronica*, 56, 93n, 95n, 96, 100, 119, 172, 173-4, 175
Guisborough, Walter of, 16, 26, 44, 174

Hainault, Guillaume, count of, 127
Hainault, Jean of, 127, 131-2, 139n, 174
Harcla, Andrew, earl of Carlisle, 86-7, 89, 95n, 102, 110, 112, 114-15, 119, 120-1, 122
Hardyng, John, 174
Hastings, John, lord, 27, 28
Hay, Gilbert de la, constable of Scotland, 19, 21
Hereford, Humphrey Bohun, earl of, 68, 69, 84-5, 111, 114-15
Hilton, Robert of, 97
Horseley, Roger, 98-100
Hotham, John de, bishop of Ely, 104-5
Hume, David, of Godscroft, 157

Isabelle, Queen of England, 104-6, 111, 127-8, 129, 147, 149, 150-1

Joan of the Tower, 149, 150
John XXII, Pope, 98, 101-2, 108-9, 119

Keith, Alexander, 125
Keith, Isabella, 157
Keith, Robert, Marischal of Scotland, 52, 69, 71-2, 78, 98-9, 157
Keith, William, of Galston, 100, 160, 163, 165
Kent, Edmund, earl of, 130
Knighton, Henry, 140, 174

Lamberton, William, bishop of St Andrews, 3-5, 9, 10-15, 18, 20, 30, 51, 101, 126, 149, 175
Lancaster, Henry, earl of, 130, 132, 139n

Lancaster, Thomas, earl of, 103, 106, 110-15, 121, 130, 175
Lanercost Chronicle, 61, 173
Lauder, Robert, 149
Lavington, Thomas de, 166-7, 168
Le Baker, Geoffrey, 166-8
Le Bel, Jean, 94n, 131, 133, 134, 135n, 138, 140n, 141, 160, 166, 168, 172, 174-5
Ledhouse, Sim of, 60, 61n, 64-5
Lennox, Malcolm, earl of, 17, 19, 25, 26, 42, 51, 84
Lindsay, Alexander, 45, 124
Lintalee, 90-3, 175
Linton, Bernard, Chancellor of Scotland, 108
Logan, Robert, 160, 164
Logan, Walter, 160, 164
Lorne, John Macdowel of, 23-4, 49-51
Lothian, 47, 57, 58, 62-3, 115
Loudon Hill, battle of, 37-8, 40n, 41
Lowrison, Twynam, 159

Macalpine line, 1
Macdowel family, 23, 24, 25, 49
Macdowel, Alexander, *see* Argyll
Macdowel, Dougal, 29
Macdowel, John, *see* Lorne
Manners, Robert, 146
Mar, Donald, earl of, 17, 131, 136, 139, 149
March, Patrick IV of Dunbar, earl of, 47
March, Patrick V of Dunbar, earl of, 47n, 63, 81, 144, 149
Marmeduke, Richard, 95-6
Melton, William, archbishop of York, 104-5
Methven, battle of, 20-1, 37, 48
Moray, Thomas Randolph, earl of, 18, 39, 48-9, 52, 69, 70, 71, 75, 77, 85, 102, 110, 115, 129, 130-1, 146, 149, 151, 152n, 164, 174
  captured by Douglas, 47-8
  tergiversations of, 47

INDEX

created earl of Moray, 63
captures Edinburgh Castle, 65, 87
victory by St Ninian's, 72-4, 77
regent-designate, 85, 102-3
and capture of Berwick, 98-100
partnership with Douglas, 104-5, 107, 112-14, 131, 137
raids in England, 107-8, 112
at Byland, 117-18
diplomatic activities, 125, 126-7
in Weardale, 134-43
and marriage of Prince David, 150-1
Mortimer, Roger, lord of Chirk, 111-12, 113
Mortimer, Roger, lord of Wigmore, 111-12, 113, 127-8, 129, 132, 147, 149, 150, 174
Mowbray, Alexander, 110
Mowbray, John, 36, 37, 113
Mowbray, Philip, 61, 80, 102
Murimuth, Adam, 126, 174
Murray, Andrew, 2, 18, 148
Murray, David, bishop of Moray, 18, 42
Myton, Chapter of, 104-5, 106, 174

Neville, Ellen, 97n
Neville, Ralph, 97, 113n, 114, 175
Neville, Robert, 'The Peacock of the North', 95-7
Northampton, Treaty of, 149
Northumberland, 58-9, 83, 95, 100, 146

Osmin, 163-4

Pass of Brander, 49-50, 118n
Pembroke, Aymer de Valence, earl of, 19-21, 30n, 35-8, 40, 41, 44, 68, 103, 111, 113, 117
Percy, Henry, lord (father), 28
Percy, Henry, lord (son), 146
Philip IV, King of France, 3

Ramsay, Alexander, 157
Randolph, Thomas, *see* Moray

Rathlin, 26, 27
Richmond, John of Brittany, earl of, 12, 41, 44, 93-4, 113, 117-119
Richmond, Thomas, 92-3
Robert I, King of Scots, 10, 12, 15, 19, 24, 25, 29, 30, 33, 35n, 41, 43, 46, 47, 49, 56, 63, 65, 66, 84, 85, 89, 94n, 98, 99, 103, 104, 106, 112, 113, 120, 126, 131, 144, 146, 150, 155, 156, 163, 165, 166, 168, 173
character, 22, 128, 152
early career, 11
killing of Comyn, 13-14
receives Douglas, 16-17
coronation, 17-18, 149
defeated at Methven, 20-1
defeated at Dalry, 24
disappearance from Scotland (1306), 26
return to Scotland (1307), 27-8
achievements in Galloway, 35
victory at Loudon Hill, 37-8, 40
strategy, 39-40, 57, 62
in north of Scotland, 42, 44-5
conquest of Argyll, 47-51
raiding policy, 58-9, 83, 130-1
captures Perth, 60-1
preparations for Bannockburn, 68-9, 70-1
at Bannockburn, 72-9
policy after Bannockburn, 82-3
siege of Carlisle, 86-7
and Papacy, 98-9, 101-2, 108-9, 151
and invasion (1322), 115
victory at Byland, 117-19
truces with England, 57, 108, 122, 129
grants to Douglas family, 122-6
succession provisions, 84-5, 102-103
invades Northumberland, 146
concludes Treaty of Northampton, 147-9
Parliaments:
St Andrews (1309), 51-2

INDEX

Robert I, King of Scots, Parliaments:—*contd.*
  Ayr (1312), 58
  Cambuskenneth (1314), 84
  Ayr (1315), 84
  Scone (1318), 102
  Edinburgh (1328), 149
  pilgrimage to Whithorn, 151-2
  last request to Douglas, and death, 152-4
Rokesby, Thomas of, 134-5
Ros, William de, 91, 175
Ross, William, earl of, 28, 49, 51, 149, 157n

St Bride's Church, Douglas, 32-3, 165
St John, John, 45
Scaithmoor, 88-9
Seton, Christopher, 17, 21, 28
Sinclair, John, 160
Sinclair, William, of Roslin, 160, 164, 167
Soules, John, 88, 89, 102
Soules, William, lord, 95, 110
Spalding, Peter (Sim) of, 98-9, 100n
Steward, James the, 3, 7, 12, 19, 41, 43, 51, 69
Steward, Walter the, 69, 75-6, 85, 89, 102, 103, 110n, 112, 117-118, 131, 157
Stewart, Alexander, of Bonkle, 48-9, 144n
Stewart, Andrew, 12, 20, 69n
Stewart, James, 131
Stewart, John, of Bonkle, 44, 48
Stewart, John, son of James the Steward, 102

Stewart, John of Bonkle, earl of Angus, *see* Angus
Stewart, Robert, later Robert II, 102, 157n
Stirling Castle, 1, 3, 58, 60, 61, 80
Strathearn, Malise, earl of, 19, 26n
Sully, Henri, seigneur de, 119, 122, 126
Surrey, William de Warenne, earl of, 57, 113, 116

Teba de Hardales, 162-4
Thirlwall, captain of Douglas Castle, 40, 42, 43
Thomas of Brotherton, earl of Norfolk, 132, 139n
Topcliff, Richard, 112-13
Trokelowe, John, 104, 128, 174

Ughtred, Thomas, 118
Ulster, Richard de Burgh, earl of, 56
Umfraville, Ingram, 3, 46, 77

Valence, Aymer de, *see* Pembroke
Vita Edwardi Secundi, 60, 61n, 104-5, 174

Wake, Thomas, lord, 130
Wallace, William, 2, 4-5, 7, 11, 12-13, 22, 44, 76, 148
Weardale campaign, 132-45, 174
Webbiton, John of, 42-3
Wemyss, Michael, 19
William I, King of Scots, 11n
Wishart, Robert, bishop of Glasgow, 10, 17, 18, 20, 85, 148
Wyntoun, Andrew, 173